PRECEPTS FOR LIVING®

PASTOR'S EDITION

Urban Ministries, Inc.
The African American Christian Publishing & Communications Co.

UMI ANNUAL COMMENTARY

PRECEPTS FOR LIVING®

PASTOR'S EDITION

MISSION STATEMENT

We are called
of God to create, produce, and distribute
quality Christian education products;
to deliver exemplary customer service;
and to provide quality Christian
educational services, which will empower
God's people, especially within the Black
community, to evangelize, disciple,
and equip people for serving Christ,
His kingdom, and church.

PRECEPTS FOR LIVING® 2019–2020
PASTOR'S EDITION
VOLUME 12
UMI (URBAN MINISTRIES, INC.)

Melvin Banks Sr., LittD, Founder and Chairman
C. Jeffrey Wright, JD, CEO

ISBN-13: 978-1-68353-347-4

Publisher: UMI (Urban Ministries, Inc.), Chicago, IL 60643.

To place an order, call us at
1-800-860-8642 or visit our website at www.urbanministries.com

Dear Pastor,

Is it your desire to see the people of God increase in their knowledge of His Will, love Him deeply, and follow Him more faithfully? Certainly you'll say "yes" because this is the drumbeat of your heart as a pastor!

It's also why UMI exists. God impressed Hosea 4:6 upon me as a boy in Birmingham, Alabama. The truth of that text resulted in my pioneering the establishment of UMI. Hosea 4:6 (NKJV) still rings true today:

"My people are destroyed for lack of knowledge."

This is also why we produce a *Precepts For Living®* Pastor's Edition. We want you to encourage your entire congregation—not just the Sunday School crowd!—to make Bible study a priority during the week. Whether it's at Sunday School, midweek Bible study, another small group gathering, or family devotions, God's people profit from regular exposure to His Word.

Precepts For Living® Pastor's Edition enables you, as pastor, to preach one or more Sunday sermons based on the International Bible Lessons. By doing this, you help strengthen each congregant in his or her understanding and application of God's Word.

We envision this *Precepts For Living®* Pastor's Edition being used along with the *Precepts For Living®* Annual Commentary. The sermons in this volume correlate with the Bible studies in *Precepts For Living®*. That way your sermons can be reinforced by Bible studies in Sunday School or other small groups. In this edition, we anticipate that you will appreciate these sermons presented as outlines and full texts. Additionally, we have included a sampling of sermons for special days. Even if you choose to develop your own sermon from the weekly Bible text, we believe this edition will prove invaluable and will certainly be a catalyst for your preaching.

You will be amazed and delighted at the impact this material will make on your entire congregation. Your church will study a Bible passage and then hear you preach on the same theme or related Bible text.

So enjoy *Precepts For Living®* Pastor's Edition and consider preaching one or more sermons based on the themes or texts. Let us know the result it makes in your congregation.

Sincerely,

Melvin E. Banks Sr, Litt.D.

Melvin E. Banks Sr., LittD

PRECEPTS FOR LIVING®

PASTOR'S EDITION

To maximize your entire congregations' biblical learning experience, this resource will help you correlate some of your sermons with companion Bible studies in the *Precepts For Living®, Annual Commentary*. The continuity between the sermons and the *Precepts* lessons will give further insight into the God-intended meaning of the Scriptures so that your Bible students can successfully understand the principles taught and apply them to their daily living. There are outlines for topical use as well.

LESSON SERMONS

LESSON SERMONS

PAGE	SERMON TITLE	SCRIPTURE	*PRECEPTS FOR LIVING®*
45	My Desire Is to Please Him	Matthew 4:1–11	February 2, 2020
47	What Not to Do	Matthew 6:1–8	February 9, 2020
49	The Disciple's Prayer	Matthew 6:9–15	February 16, 2020
51	Keep At It!	Luke 11:5-13	February 23, 2020
53	Called to Accountability	Amos 5:18–24	March 1, 2020
55	Do I Matter?	Habakkuk 1:1–4, 12–14	March 8, 2020
57	Two Birds, One Stone	Habakkuk 2:6–14	March 15, 2020
59	The More Important Things	Micah 3:1–3, 9-12; 6:6–8	March 22, 2020
61	Leading by God's Example	Malachi 2:1–9; 3:5–6	March 29, 2020
63	A Servant for All	Isaiah 42:1–9	April 5, 2020
65	The Power of the Resurrection	1 Corinthians 15:1–8, 12-14, 20–23, 42–45	April 12, 2020
67	Boomerang Season	Esther 7:1–10	April 19, 2020
69	What God Loves the Most	Isaiah 61:8–11; 62:2–4	April 26, 2020
71	God's Lullaby	Zephaniah 3:14–20	May 3, 2020
73	No Justice., No Peace	Zechariah 8:1–8, 11–17	May 10, 2020
75	Temporary Fix	Jeremiah 21:8–14	May 17, 2020
77	Evil Kings, Beware!	Jeremiah 22:1–10	May 24, 2020
79	Return to God Again	Hosea 11:1–2, 7–10; 12:1–2, 6–14	May 31, 2020
81	Living in the Rhythm of Wisdom	Proverbs 1:1–4, 7–8, 10–11, 20–22, 32–33	June 7, 2020
83	The Treasure of Wisdom	Proverbs 2:1–11	June 14, 2020
85	The Guiding Light of Wisdom	Proverbs 8:8–14, 17–21	June 21, 2020
87	The Nourishment of Wisdom	Proverbs 9:1–6, 8–10, 13–18	June 28, 2020
89	Vindication of Wisdom in the Wilderness	Matthew 11:7–19	July 5, 2020
92	The Wisdom of a Child	Ecclesiastes 3:1, 7; Luke 2:39–52	July 12, 2020
94	Familiarity Breeds Contempt	Mark 6:1–6	July 19, 2020
96	The Wise Way to True Life	John 14:1–14	July 26, 2020
98	Rejoice! Endure! Pray!	James 1:1–11	August 2, 2020
100	Hearing and Doing the World	James 1:19–27	August 9, 2020
102	What Makes Our Faith Come Alive	James 2:14-26	August 16, 2020
104	Words Have Meaning and Consequences	James 3:1–12	August 23, 2020
106	Wisdom as Walking Faith	James 3:13–18; 5:7–12	August 30, 2020

Contributors

Rev. John Burton Jr., MDiv, Contributing Writer for Precepts for Living, Pastor's Edition and Jesus and Me (JAM)

Rev. Jaimie D. Crumley, STM, PhD Student at University of California, Los Angeles

Pastor Gabby Cudjoe-Wilkes, MDiv, Co-Pastor at The Double Love Experience, Brooklyn, NY

Pastor Jerome Gay, Jr., Lead Pastor at Vision Church, Raleigh, NC

Emmanuel Ephraim, MDiv, Associate Pastor at First Baptist Church, Laurel, MD

Rev. Wayne C. Hopkins, MAT, Pastor at First Timothy Missionary Baptist Church, Los Angeles, CA

Rev. Matthew C. Jones, DMin, Lead Pastor at Del Rey Church, Playa Del Rey, CA

Rev. Terence K. Leathers, DMin, Pastor at Mount Vernon Church, Clayton, NC

Pastor Emeritus Stan Long, DDiv, Founder of South Bay Community Church and member of the Board of Directors at UMI

Ramon Mayo, MA, Senior Innovation Analyst at UMI

Marvin McMickle, PhD, President and Professor of African American Religious Studies at Colgate Rochester Crozer Divinity School, Rochester, NY

Pastor Tony Myles, MM, Pastor at Riverside Church, Big Lake, MN

Pastor Geno Olison, Senior Pastor at South Suburban Vineyard Church, Chicago, IL

Rev. Cheryl L. Price, PhD, Vice President of Content at UMI

Gina A. S. Robinson, MDiv, PhD student at Garrett-Evangelical Theological Seminary

Allen Reynolds, MDiv, Innovation Analyst at UMI

Contributors

Jeremias Santos, MATS, Contributing Writer for Precepts for Living Pastors Edition

---

Rev. Christian Savage, MDiv, Senior Pastor at New Mount Olive AME Church, Chesapeake, VA

Dr. R. Neal Siler, Senior Pastor at First Shiloh Baptist Church, Mechanicsville, VA, and director of The Healing Place Center for Counseling and Spiritual Formation

---

Pastor Tommy E. Smith Jr., Senior Pastor at Palma Ceia Baptist Church, Hayward, CA

Howard Lee Thomas III, MDiv, Church Planter at Oikos Church, Houston, TX

Rev. Porsha D. Williams, M Div, Pastor to Youth and Children at Bethany Baptist Church, Newark, NJ

Rev. Kathy Williamson, MDiv, Education Committee Chair with WOCIM and Associate Minister at Mount Aery Baptist Church, Bridgeport, CT

A LOOK AT THE ELDERS OF ANTIOCH

Acts 11:18–26; 13:1–3
by Marvin A. McMickle, PhD

The origins of the Christian church can be traced to the city of Antioch in Syria, where church leaders fled when persecution of Christians became too intense in Jerusalem. From Antioch, Paul began the first of his three missionary journeys to spread the Gospel to the nations of Asia Minor and southern Europe. There in Antioch, Paul and Barnabas were ordained and sent forth to that work of evangelism by the authority of Simeon the Niger and Lucius of Cyrene.

There is something interesting and important about the church in the city of Antioch, something that historians and filmmakers seem to have overlooked or completely ignored. It has to do with the ethnic and cultural and regional composition of the church in Antioch 2,000 years ago. Acts 13 mentions the names of four men who were among the elders, or spiritual leaders, of that early Christian community. People from all over the world are quite familiar with two of those names: Barnabas and Saul. Every Sunday school student has heard something about both of those apostles. Their names are just as well known to us as the names of the Lord's first disciples Peter, James, John, and the others.

However, there were two other names mentioned in Acts 13 that seem to have been completely forgotten or overlooked or relegated to the trash heap of history. Nevertheless, there they are for all to notice: Simeon who was called Niger and Lucius of Cyrene. Who do you suppose these two men were, and what is important to us about their presence in the Bible? Simeon was called Niger. That is a Latin word that means black or dark. So, we know there was a leader in the church at Antioch whose skin color was so conspicuous that he was called Niger. He was a black man in the language of the modern day. The other man was Lucius from Cyrene. That was a city from the North African country that is now known as Libya.

Consider that the leaders of the church at Antioch not only included the two well-known characters of Paul and Barnabas, but also included one man who was referred to as Niger and another man whose homeland is identified as the region of North Africa. Indeed, according to Acts 13, it was Simeon and Lucius who ordained and consecrated Paul and Barnabas. The text says they "laid their hands on them, they sent them away" (Acts 13:3).

Do you not find it strange that the names of Simeon and Lucius are seldom, if ever, mentioned in most churches? Paul and Barnabas have churches, schools, and hospitals named after them. Meanwhile, nothing has been done to establish forever the names of Simeon the Niger and Lucius of Cyrene. Let me point out to you that these two men and their ethnic identity were not inserted into the Bible long after the book of Acts had been completed. They were not an afterthought. Their names were not inserted in the Bible during the Civil Rights Movement. There was no US Supreme Court order that mandated that these names be included as a form of Affirmative Action. These names, and the link they certify between black people and biblical faith, have been in the Book of Acts from the beginning. But for all this time they have been largely overlooked, if not completely ignored. It is important for us to **Take a Look at the Elders of Antioch.**

Let me state several reasons this observation is important. First, this single text helps us dispel the Gospel according to Cecil B. DeMille, the Hollywood filmmaker. Has it ever occurred to you that all his epic films about biblical stories relegate black people to obscurity? Consider the most notable example of excluding black people from the biblical story, *The Ten Commandments*. How likely do you think it is that Moses really looked like Charlton Heston, or that Rameses looked like Yul Brenner? What filmmakers cannot undo in 1958 is what we see written here in Acts 13 that dates to around 60 AD. The Gospel according to Cecil B. DeMille is not the authorized version. Black people have played a leading role in the Bible for thousands of years.

A second equally important point for us is the reminder that our history as a people does not begin in the cotton and tobacco fields of North and South America and the Caribbean. Long before we came to this hemisphere, African people had established countries and great civilizations. Slavery in America may be part of the history of some African people, but our history certainly does not begin at that point.

The people of Africa are much more interested in shaking off the last vestiges of European colonial rule on the African continent that ended just forty years ago, than they are in what happened to those Africans who were taken away, never to return, four hundred years ago. When you go to Africa, you become reconnected to the cultures that existed on that continent while Europe was still groping through the Dark Ages. Empires such as Songhay and Mali were centers of art, learning, and organized religion long before the trans-Atlantic slave trade began. They were a civilized and ordered community whose darkness only began when they were forced into slavery. Let it never be forgotten that our history does not begin in America; it is rooted in the continent of Africa. The presence of Simeon the Niger and Lucius of Cyrene is also a reminder of that fact.

A third reason I am intrigued by the presence of Simeon and Lucius is that it helps me refute those who continue to insist that Christianity is "the white man's religion." Some would suggest that it was white Christians who were responsible for the brutality inflicted upon black people over the years. That point may be largely true. However, it does not dismiss the presence of Simon and Lucius as leaders of the church at Antioch. Black people—African people—have been a part of the Christian faith from the very beginning, as the Ethiopian Orthodox Church and the Coptic Church can attest. I do not doubt, and I cannot refute the claim, that much of the worst of slavery was done with the full knowledge and support of some organized groups of white Christians. However, many white Christians also fought and died to end slavery both in America and in Europe. Black people are not out of touch with their history when they confess faith in Jesus Christ. They have been doing that since Simeon the Niger and Lucius of Cyrene were among the elders at Antioch in the first century AD.

My fourth and final point is this: the story in Acts 13 must serve as a challenge to the modern-day Christian church around the world. You and I are members of a church that carries the name of the place where people were first called Christians. Wouldn't it be great of we looked and acted like those whose name we bear into the twenty-first century? It seems that racism has caused us to digress from the organizational style of the church at Antioch. Notice that Saul and Barnabas, along with Simeon and Lucius served as leaders in that church. How many churches today have leadership that looks like that? Not many, I would imagine. Rather than having interracial leadership, we can barely sustain a handful of interracial memberships in our churches across the country. How sad that we have reverted to our present state of racial separation.

Let me remind us all that God gave the church in the United States another opportunity to look like the early church in Antioch. It was within our reach between 1909 and 1914. Did you know that between 1909 and 1914 there were over 300 white preachers who had been ordained into the Church of God in Christ and who looked to C. H. Mason as their bishop? In 1912 when race riots were tearing this country apart and when what Billie Holliday called "the strange fruit" of black bodies were hanging from trees after being lynched by white mobs, God gave us a chance to look like the church in Antioch.

The problem was that the social pressures were too much for those white clergy. In 1914 the body of Christ that could have been such a witness to the country at that time was once again divided because of racism and the assumptions of white supremacy. The white preachers ordained by a black bishop could not or would not submit to the authority of a black man, so they left COGIC and went out and formed the Assemblies of God. I invite you to look at their statement of origin on their website and see how history has once again been erased and rewritten. They do not mention William Seymour, black leader of the Azusa Street revival, or C. H. Mason, the black preacher who ordained every single white person who organized the Assemblies of God in 1914. They just give the impression that they sprouted up all by themselves.

Here again is the problem that stands between blacks and whites in the church and in the world: the present arrangement is built upon lies, distortions, half-truths and omissions. Integrating our churches is not something we need to attempt for the first time in the twenty-first century. It is something that we need to reclaim from the church at Antioch in the very first century AD. And we must remember that integration is not the real issue. The real issue is the equality of all persons. When Paul in Acts 17 says to the Greeks in Athens, "From one blood God made all nations of men to dwell together on the face of the earth," he may have had his friendship with Simeon and Lucius on his mind. When he said in Galatians 3, "There is neither Jew nor Gentile," he might have had Simeon and Lucius on his mind.

How sad that this is not yet not true with all Christian bodies. How and why have we built these self-imposed divisions among ourselves? How did we get to this state of disunity? Surely the church of the twenty-first century can learn from the church of the first century when it comes to diversity and inclusion. Would it not be a wonderful thing if every congregation was a place where Paul and Barnabas along with Simon the Niger and Lucius of Cyrene could sit and serve together?

We might as well learn how to live and work and worship down here on earth, because the Bible says nothing about separate sections in heaven. There will be no black section over here and no white section over there. There will be no all-male section over here and all-female over there. There will not even be a Baptist section over here for those that have been through the baptism of bodily immersion in water, and no Methodist section over there for those that have been "dry cleaned."

I know the story of the African Methodist Episcopal Church where Richard Allen, Absalom Jones, and others were present in worship but had paused for prayer at a spot where their ethnicity did not permit them to be. I know they were dragged from their knees in a white church and then went out with Jones forming St. Thomas Episcopal Church with Allen establishing the AME Church. There might never have been all these black denominations today if white Christians in the eighteenth and nineteenth century had known about Simeon and Lucius and made room for their black brothers and sisters.

I know the story of John Street Methodist Episcopal Church in New York City in 1796. I know about Peter Williams, Sr. and James Varick, who stood up for the right of black clergy to exercise their gifts for ministry that the white Methodist Episcopal Church had disallowed. I know what happened in 1821, when the African Methodist Episcopal Zion Church was organized. I know that the AME Zion Church has been called the Freedom Church, because Frederick Douglass, Sojourner Truth, Harriet Tubman, and Paul Robeson were shaped and molded in the Zion Church. I know all of that, and I honor and salute all of that.

I know the story of the Christian Methodist Episcopal Church in 1870 and how they were established by a group of whites in Jackson, Tennessee who found it easier to aid in organizing a black denomination than to simply admit the former slaves as members of their Southern Methodist Episcopal Church. I know that the American Baptist Church split in two around 1841 over the issue of slavery and over the role that Black people would be allowed to play in that church. I know that the Southern Baptist Church was fully complicit in the perpetuation of slavery, Jim Crow, segregation, and in the continuation of a biblical justification for the subordination of Black people. I also know that they only very recently acknowledged the truth of what I just said. And let me say, issuing a statement from the annual convention is a far cry from opening their most prestigious churches, not just for black membership, but also for black leadership in the pulpit and the pew.

However, I know one thing more. I know about the church at Antioch in Syria. I know they were first called Christians there, and they began in a place to which we should be trying to return. They commissioned Paul and Barnabas to their ministry as missionaries for Jesus Christ. And I know that on that ordination council, among the elders at Antioch were two black men: Simeon the Niger and Lucius of Cyrene. If the church had kept their names alive, history would have been very different. We would have known about the black presence in the Bible. We would have known that our history did not begin in slavery but with great and cultured societies in Africa. Finally, we would have known that from the Day of Pentecost in Acts to the commissioning of Paul and Barnabas in Acts 13, the church of Jesus Christ began as an interracial and an intercultural community. I do not know if we will ever have the courage and the audacity to commit ourselves to getting back to that kind of church.

I do know this, however: this life is not all there is for those who put our faith in Christ. I know that God has something waiting for the faithful on the other side of this earthly journey. I know that weeping may endure for an evening, but that joy will come in the morning. And in that heavenly home, in that house not made with hands, there will be the descendants of Paul and Barnabas, and the descendants of Simeon the Niger and Lucius of Cyrene. "*When we all get to heaven what a day of rejoicing that will be. When we all see Jesus, we'll sing and shout the victory.*"

Sermon Evaluation Form

At Urban Ministries, Inc., we strive to provide resources that assist in developing and training students, pastors, and preachers to write and deliver sermons that display

- Faithfulness to Scripture
- Concern for the World
- Authenticity from the Messenger
- and Transformative Power

We created this sermon evaluation to serve as a tool for you to assess a given sermon, whether it be yours, a colleague's, or a student's. This tool can be utilized to evaluate either a written or preached sermon.

Ratings: 1 - Outstanding; 2 - Great; 3 - Good; 4 - Satisfactory; 5 - Unsatisfactory

Preacher's Name

____

Sermon Title

____

Name of Church

____

Scripture Passage

____

Date

____

1. Faithfulness to Scripture

The sermons should be faithful to the words of the text and should provide evidence of close engagement with the main points and issues of it. The sermons should cohere to the larger narrative of God's revelation in Scripture.

Ratings: 1 - Outstanding; 2 - Great; 3 - Good; 4 - Satisfactory; 5 - Unsatisfactory

Section 1

The sermon content demonstrated faithful engagement with Scripture.

1 2 3 4 5

The sermon content illuminated God's presence in the text.

1 2 3 4 5

The sermon content helped you understand the Scripture.

1 2 3 4 5

The sermon content connected the text to God's presence and action in the larger biblical narrative.

1 2 3 4 5

Section 2

Was a main point in the text clearly presented in the sermon? If so, please state your understanding of the main point based on the sermon:

____
____
____
____
____
____
____
____

2. Concern for World (Contextual)

The sermon should connect God's presence and activity in the text to the issues in today's world. The sermon should address how the message can be understood in the light of the major social and personal challenges of the listeners.

Ratings: 1 - Outstanding; 2 - Great; 3 - Good; 4 - Satisfactory; 5 - Unsatisfactory

Section 1

The sermon content demonstrated an awareness of today's major issues.

1 2 3 4 5

The sermon content showed a clear connection from the message of the text to a particular problem or issue in the world.

1 2 3 4 5

The sermon content drew appropriate and useful analogies between the biblical world and contemporary society/culture.

1 2 3 4 5

You felt empowered by the sermon to address the concerns in the world or your community.

1 2 3 4 5

Section 2

Please list an example or two of how the sermon resonated with the social context(s) of today's world.

____
____
____
____
____
____
____
____

3. Authenticity of the Messenger

The writer or preacher of the sermon should demonstrate that the message in Scripture has convicted him or her at a personal level. Thus, personal engagement and thoughtfulness should be evident in the sermon, with the preacher conveying an authentic voice.

Ratings: 1 - Outstanding; 2 - Great; 3 - Good; 4 - Satisfactory; 5 - Unsatisfactory

Section 1

The preacher approached the text in a genuine way.

1 2 3 4 5

A consistent voice or perspective was presented in an authentic way.

1 2 3 4 5

The preacher conveyed personal engagement and deep thoughtfulness on the text.

1 2 3 4 5

The preacher demonstrated conviction and passion for the topic and text.

1 2 3 4 5

Section 2

Please elaborate on the sense of authenticity you received from the preacher. What confirmed that the messenger was engaged and connected to the text?

____
____
____
____
____

4. Transformative Power

The sermons should challenge, encourage, and strengthen your congregation in their attempts to become faithful disciples of Jesus. Message points should use illustrations or scenarios that are relevant and meet listeners' experiences in their daily living. The explication of the text should be easy to apply to any number of situations.

Ratings: 1 - Outstanding; 2 - Great; 3 - Good;

4 - Satisfactory; 5 - Unsatisfactory

Section 1

The sermon content was relevant for challenging, encouraging, and strengthening believers in their journey of Christian discipleship.

1 2 3 4 5

The sermon content lends itself to transformational living for believers.

1 2 3 4 5

The sermons addressed a specific area of life that relates to faithfully living as a believer.

1 2 3 4 5

The sermons contained the potential to be life-changing for a wide range of listeners.

1 2 3 4 5

Section 2

Please comment briefly on the potential for transformative power of the sermon.

____
____
____
____
____
____
____

5. Sermon Delivery

If applicable, evaluate the preacher on his or her delivery of the given sermon using the following:

Ratings: 1 - Outstanding; 2 - Great; 3 - Good;
4 - Satisfactory; 5 - Unsatisfactory

Section 1

The preacher held a posture and used body language that was fitting for the content of the message.

1 2 3 4 5

The preacher delivered the sermon in a clear and understandable tone of voice, and showed variation at appropriate points to place emphasis.

1 2 3 4 5

The preacher conveyed a strong sense of confidence in the message and the delivery.

1 2 3 4 5

The preacher effectively connected to the congregation with consistent eye-contact.

1 2 3 4 5

The preacher showed a deep level of engagement with the message by not simply reading but making it come alive.

Section 2

Please comment the strengths and weaknesses you noticed in the delivery of the sermon.

____

Even When You Are Not, God Is Faithful

By Dr. R. Neal Siler

Lesson Theme	Unit Theme	Scripture
Faith and Doubt	God Is Faithful	Genesis 19:1, 15–26, 29

INTRODUCTION

God must have been madly in love with Lot and his family. Lot lived in a place of great wickedness. By his living on the periphery of the city, as the Scripture says (Genesis 12:12), we may infer he knew of the evilness of this place, but something held him there. The strangers that appeared were on assignment to rescue Lot and his family. Lot was not made for this place or the wickedness and debauchery it invited. I wonder how many times he had tried to get out but felt helpless and stuck in a place of his own choosing—feeling like he could not do differently or live differently because of the choices he had made.

MESSAGE POINTS

Message Point 1: "God Is Not Willing to Give Up on You" (Genesis 15:15)
You may feel trapped, but that feeling is inconsistent with God's nature not to give up on you. You may feel your back is against the wall and you are at a place in your life you can't get out of. It's a desert place, with no water in sight and no one to offer you refreshment. Maybe you feel the sting of compromise in your life where decisions and plans only lead to despair and darkness. Hear this! God is not giving up on you! We don't know if these were the only messengers or if there were messengers before. What we do know is that God did not give up on Lot, and God won't give up on you! Your sense of foreboding is your awareness of God's desires for you. You feel God is disappointed with your life, because you were not made for this place. The people you've connected with in no way reflect the character of the God you used to be so in love with. You feel compromised in your personal, professional, and spiritual life. You are just in a dark place, surrounded by people intent on doing dark deeds. But there's good news today. God has sent a messenger to rescue you. Hear the message—"You can't stay here; you don't belong here!"

Message Point 2: "Don't Resist Your Deliverance" (v. 16)
Sin captures you and holds you in a life you were not designed for. But you can stand in God's grace despite past failures. Even after the messengers told Lot what God was about to do to the city, Lot's wife looked back, not ready to exit her season of sin. The problem with sin is it touches our soul. It is hard to let it go. Lot lingered too! The messengers had to take him by the hand to lead him out. Lot had second thoughts of entertaining sin's invitation. Sin's assignment is to enslave with deadly desire and destructive consequences that cannot be undone. The wages of sin will always be death. But in the place of your greatest iniquity, God will display His greatest faithfulness. That's why we can stand in God's grace despite past failures and struggles.

Message Point 3: "God's Faithfulness Is Stronger than Our Infidelity" (vv. 17, 22)

Just as God really loved Lot, God really loves you! And rising from the depths of your disappointment and compromise is an ever-so-vague memory of what your life can be like. A stranger appears, out of nowhere, and begins to talk and act in a way reminiscent of your lost hopes and dreams. Suddenly, the vacant parts of your life are filled with hope again as you hear these words, "You can't stay here; you don't belong here." You awaken to God's faithfulness and realize He has been holding you all along, waiting for you to trust His deliverance. How many times have you felt the stirring and heard His voice, only to ignore it? God's faithfulness has always been stronger than your infidelity. Nothing you have experienced is enough for you to turn your back against God; He is the only lasting source of life that can satisfy the desires of your heart. Don't look back, don't linger. Run!

THAT'LL PREACH

Arthur Winston was an African American who worked for the Los Angeles Metropolitan Transportation Authority for seventy-two years. He never missed a single day of work except to attend the funeral of his wife Francis, in 1988. At 100 years old, he was recognized as the most reliable worker the US Department of Labor had ever known. In 1996, President Bill Clinton awarded him an Employee of the Century citation for his work ethic and dedication. Arthur Winston was a faithful worker, someone his company could count on. Today we focus on the faithfulness of God. He is eternally faithful.

- Psalm 36:5 describes His faithfulness as higher than the heavens.
- Psalm 40:10 says, "I have not hid thy righteousness within my heart; I have declared thy faithfulness and thy salvation: I have not concealed thy lovingkindness and thy truth from the great congregation."
- Psalm 89:5 says, "The heavens shall praise thy wonders, O LORD: thy faithfulness also in the congregation of the saints."

CONCLUSION

God is madly in love with you. God showers you with new mercies every day. We all could testify that we've been in some "Lot-like" situations. God has delivered us in the past, and He will deliver us in the future. God is the answer for our greatest longings and has provided for our deepest needs even when we have been unfaithful. He is not a meantime, in-between-time God, but an all-the-time, always-faithful God. Whatever you are going through, just know that God is in pursuit of you. He will dispatch messengers to rescue you from the plight of sin. When they show up, don't linger or look back. What is behind you is deadly, but what is before you is glorious.

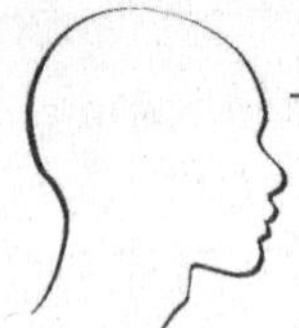

God Answers Prayer

By Kathy Williamson

Lesson Theme	Unit Theme	Scripture
God Answers Prayer	God is Faithful	1 Samuel 1:9–20

INTRODUCTION

Have you ever wanted something so badly, been faced with a situation so desperate, or had a need so great that you knew it would require the hand of God to intervene? In our Scripture, we see Hannah had such a need, a deep yearning to bear a child. This yearning was extraordinary because Hannah knew no matter how much her husband loved her, it was something he could not fulfill. She continued making her request and bargaining with God until she was confident God would grant her heart's desire. Although some may view Hannah's plea as an act of desperation, most of us can relate to Hannah's situation. Hannah believed God *could* do it, she desired God to do it, now she had to wait to see if God *would* do it.

MESSAGE POINTS

Message Point 1: "Confident Plea" (1 Samuel 1:9–11)

Hannah's anguish caused her to seek God requesting three things: see me, remember me, and grant my petition. Hannah came before the Lord, a barren woman who might have been used to being minimized by others. She was ridiculed by her husband's other wife and quite possibly by the other women in her town. And although her husband loved her, it was Peninnah who was able to bear children for him. Hannah knew in her heart that if God only saw her and remembered her, her request for a male child would be granted. She said, "O LORD of hosts, if thou wilt indeed look on the affliction of thine handmaid, and remember me, and not forget thine handmaid, but wilt give unto thine handmaid a man child." Before asking God for the child, Hannah needed God to see her. With a certainty that God could, she made a vow of her commitment to giving the child back to God. We want God to see us, to feel our infirmities, and to remember us. Of course we want our prayers to be answered, but there is a greater need to know our prayers are heard by God. Hannah's prayer shows her confidence that all things are possible when God shows up.

Message Point 2: "Confident Faith" (vv. 12–16)

Hannah's faith brings her to the Tabernacle where she continued to inquire of the Lord. Although in a public place, Hannah prayed and wept before God. She didn't pray as the hypocrites prayed to be seen by men, but she prayed in her heart so that only God knew her request. As Eli the priest stood to watch over the Tabernacle, he noticed Hannah. He took note of her mouth moving, her downtrodden appearance, and the tears flowing down her face. His assumption was that she was drunk with wine or strong drink. Hannah knew that she risked everything by praying outside the Tabernacle, but she believed the risk was worth taking. When believing God for something extraordinary, it may mean taking risks. It may come at the cost of people not understanding your faith, people doubting God's ability to fulfill your request, or even people questioning whether or not you are deserving. Eli's immediate reaction was to chastise her, calling her a wicked woman. He even went as far as to ask how long she would continue in this drunken state. Hannah was less concerned about how she appeared to those looking on than how she appeared to God. Some prayers require a boldness that causes us to put it all on the line.

Message Point 3: "Confident Reward" (vv. 17–20)

Eli realized that Hannah was, in fact, praying to God and gave her an assurance to go in peace, believing God would grant her petition. He never asked what it was she was requesting, but rather he relied on her faith. She left with the assurance that not only was God able but that God would. She had a confidence notable in what she did next. The text tells us that she ate, worshiped, and returned home. Before the manifestation of an answered prayer, there comes a time when your faith tells you that God has heard and will deliver. Hannah had such a moment. She was confident that she would receive her son. Our confidence comes once we have sought God, realize that God hears us and recognize that God sees us. Hannah named her son Samuel, which means "God hears," saying, "Because I have asked him of the LORD."

THAT'LL PREACH

We all may recall a time when we had a secret petition; one in which God was our only source and confidant. Perhaps our petition was even greater than we dared to dream. Was it to attend an Ivy League school, to acquire a certain position on a job, to start your own business or healing for yourself or a loved one? Were the odds so insurmountable that you dared not share it with others? It is in these moments that our faith is put into action.

In 1980, little Alise Williamson, then a twelve-year-old girl, dared to dream. She shared with someone she respected and admired that she desired to become a lawyer at Yale Law School. He immediately chastised her, saying to be more realistic. She immediately corrected herself stating that she would become a teacher. "That's more like it," was his reply. From that day on, Alise kept her dream between her and God, and she buried this dream deep within. Thirty-two years later, after a promising career within the judicial system, Alise had the opportunity to attend Yale Divinity School. While there, she was afforded the opportunity to take classes at Yale Law School. On her first walk down the halls, Alise was quickly reminded of her prayer over thirty years prior. Alise lived her life with a confidence that all things were possible in God. Although her prayers went from pleading to ones of gratitude for every blessing along the way, Alise had an inner assurance that God could answer her prayers. It is not our works or pleading that causes God to move, but rather our confidence in God moves us to have faith in the Lord.

CONCLUSION

When we pray, we understand that God's ways and thoughts are greater than our own. It is God the Creator who knows what is best for us. When we pray, we must pray with a confidence that God hears our petition and that God will respond. We don't always know the ending of the story, but we do know the author, and His record is sure.

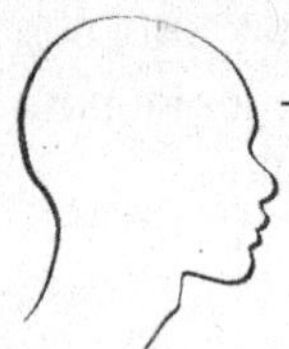

The Faithful God

By Geno Olison

Lesson Theme	Unit Theme	Scripture
Bread from Heaven	God is Faithful	Exodus 16:1–8, 13–15

INTRODUCTION

To find someone who is loyal, constant, steadfast, and reliable is a rare find. We might even find that we, ourselves, struggle to be faithful, to keep our word, to make good on our commitments, and to be someone who can be counted on especially when we don't feel like it. If you're in search of a perfect example of faithfulness, look no further than God our Father. His deep love and commitment to us is truly remarkable. His fidelity to us is most evident when we seem least deserving of His love, provision, and protection. Exodus 16 provides us with a vivid look at how God's faithfulness shines, especially when it's in contrast to the faithlessness, ingratitude, and complaining of His people. The average human would withdraw their support and generosity in the midst of such ugliness, but God shows Himself to be faithful even when His people are faithless.

MESSAGE POINTS

Message Point 1: "And the People Complained" (Exodus 16:1–3)

Complaining comes so easily, doesn't it? You don't even have to try to complain. It just happens. It's usually not thoughtful, its aim is sloppy, and complainers aren't careful to get the details right. The entire Israelite community began complaining about the unpleasant conditions of the wilderness. They complained about everything, including the accommodations and the food, and they aimed these complaints at Aaron and Moses, their leaders. This discontent was so strong that it made their time in Egyptian captivity seem like a luxury cruise. They remembered a life of ease and an abundance of delicious food that sounds more like a mirage than conditions that ever actually existed. But this is what happens when a complaining disposition takes over and we allow ourselves to sit in the brine of discontent. Our vision is skewed, and even the past is misremembered. Moses and Aaron see this and come to the conclusion that the people have an issue with God and not them. They're right. But how would God respond to such audacious ingratitude?

Message Point 2: "God Makes A Plan and a Promise" (vv. 4–8)

Despite the murmuring and complaining of a people who'd been delivered out of the hands of brutal slavery, God shows us what is arguably His best quality: His faithfulness. He is bound by His commitment to His people. He could destroy them for their lack for gratitude and for their irreverence, but He continues to make their total wellbeing His personal responsibility. With this he hatches a plan and makes a promise. The plan: supernaturally rain down bread from heaven each day and a generous supply of quail each evening. All they had to do was gather and prepare the food each day. God's plan even included a double supply on the sixth day so that they didn't have to gather on the Sabbath. What a generous God! His generosity is especially evident because this plan and promise was produced in response to the murmurs of His people. This reminds us that it's okay to be honest with God. He knows our frailty and that we often can't see what He sees. He seems to allow for our humanity and still chooses to find creative ways to give us far more than we deserve and to meet us where we are. But all of this is not just a plan or empty words. He tells His messengers, Moses and Aaron, to tell the people about this, but the real blessing is that it actually happened!

Message Point 3: "God Delivers" (vv. 13–15)

God shows His command over creation in verse 13 when a vast number of quail fly in and cover the camp in response to the promise God made to His disgruntled people. Then, as the dew evaporated the following morning, the flakey manna remained all over the ground. The people were puzzled and perplexed; Moses had to explain to them that it was God delivering on His promise. Isn't it striking how God's track record of faithfulness throughout history, and even in our lives, can still be lost on us as we go through dark seasons of discouragement? At those times, only our daily bread serves as a steady reminder that God is who He says He is and that He is bound by His promise to meet every need and to be committed to His people, even when we are undeserving. God's faithfulness means that we can count on Him, even when we complain or walk away from Him, He responds with a covenant commitment to keep His promise and hold up His end of the deal.

THAT'LL PREACH

It's interesting how people who are dishonest think everyone is lying, and how people who steal expect that others are also always looking for the opportunity to steal. People who use flattery to gain an advantage often assume that others' complements are given with a less than pure motive. At the root of this is our tendency to superimpose our character flaws onto others and consciously or unconsciously assume the worst. It's not uncommon for us to do this in our relationship with our Heavenly Father. We're acquainted with our own unreliable nature and the frequency with which we fail to make good on our promises and to fulfill our commitments. We know how many empty words we speak each day and how our faithfulness often depends on our mood or the circumstances. It can take real work for us to remember that God is not that way. He can't be less than faithful. He can't go back on His word. He can't be less than God. It is utterly impossible. Even our lack of faithfulness has no impact on how faithful God is (2 Timothy 2:13).

CONCLUSION

God's character is to be found in us. The faithfulness of God is not just something we should count on; it should be something we aspire to. God hears us, promises to meet our needs, and delivers the goods on time every time. He's a constant in the chaos and doesn't let the externals complicate who He is. We should long to be a people that God and others can count on. We should let the faithfulness of God call us higher. May God's faithfulness in our lives make us more faithful.

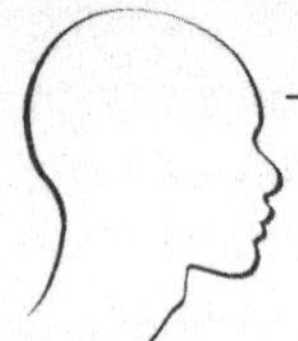

God Hears Our Cry

By Rev. Terence K. Leathers, DMin

Lesson Theme	Unit Theme	Scripture
God Hears Our Cry	God Is Faithful	Numbers 13:1–2, 17,25–28,14:1–2,5–10

INTRODUCTION

The Negro spiritual *Done Made My Vow* has a verse that speaks to the essence of this text. The verse says, "I will go, I shall go to see what the end will be." This verse is sung in response to complete reliance on and allegiance to the will and way of God. It is divine submission such that the manifestation of His desire for His leader and people will come to fruition. With this outlook, we can rest on the fact that God will have His own way and that He is the potter and we are His proverbial clay. As such, He will shape and mold us so that we stand ready to activate His mission for us and those whom He has called out to follow Him.

MESSAGE POINTS

Message Point 1: "God's Commands" (Numbers 13:1–3)
Activation of what God wanted Moses to do comes through a personal and intimate command. It is as if God and Moses are having lunch together at their favorite diner, and God says, "Moses, send some men to explore the land of Canaan." Both God and Moses are familiar with one another, and as such, Moses obeys the command without question or pause. Moses does not take a moment to consider what God is asking but takes immediate action based on God's track record with him in the past. God had brought him and the Israelites out of difficult situations. So Moses didn't mind allowing God to write another chapter about the advantages of being obedient. When you have been in close spiritual proximity to God, you can follow Him with ever greater assurance that what God has in store for you will happen. As the Cosmopolitan Church of Prayer choir sings, "God says it, I believe it. I'm going to take Him at His word."

Message Point 2: "Analyze What You See" (vv. 4–20)
Moses sends men from each tribe to explore the land and analyze what they see. This is neither a vacation nor a walk in the park to satisfy a longing to see or experience something new. They are looking for a place that they can call home. How mighty are the people that occupy the land? Can the land accommodate the needs of a growing population? What are the obstacles, human and otherwise, that prohibit occupancy? These are the questions that the Israelites must ask and answer. God's intention is to present situations to us such that we can analyze and test the premise that God will do what He says He will do.

Message Point 3: "Who's Talking What?" (Numbers 14:1–10)
Caleb and Joshua had spied out the land and had reported that it was good, and in spite of the obstacles, it could be occupied. But the murmurings became louder and more pronounced. The Children of Israel indicated that their

plight would have been better had they stayed in Egypt. In Egypt, they were aware of who they were and their place in society. Egypt was comfortable, familiar, and non-threatening. Unlike this new land, Egypt did not challenge them. Egypt allowed them to be content with the status quo. But if they were to occupy this new land, it would demand their total trust in God and those who would lead them. The Israelites must remember whom they listened to even while they were in moments of uncertainty coupled with negative thoughts about their future. Moses was God's mouthpiece and spoke assurance to the children of Israel. When we go through the hard transitions of life, we must be in fellowship and communication with those who will speak God's assurance into our life.

THAT'LL PREACH

Often in our lives, we are forced to seek out new horizons. Our spiritual brooks have dried up. Our familiar environments are no longer working for us. They no longer suit our demeanor or address the possibilities of what God wants us to be. In those times, we must have a relationship with Jesus that will help us navigate the transitions of life. Even when those transitions are hard, we must hold onto His hand. Even if those transitions cause others to question what we believe to be destiny or the land flowing with milk and honey, we must hold onto His hand. Even if those transitions cause us to rethink some relationships and set others aside, we must hold onto His hand. One thing about holding onto God's hand is that it will comfort you in unfamiliar territory, and you can squeeze a little harder should you need a little more assurance. The hymn says, "Hold (onto his hand) to God's unchanging hand, Hold (onto his hand) to God's unchanging hand, Build your hopes on things eternal, Hold to God's unchanging hand." The lesson is that God will be there to hold your hand even when the brooks are gone.

CONCLUSION

As we encounter life, let us remember that God has something for us to do. He gives a command for our lives. Our natural instinct will be to analyze what we see and count the obstacles. But if we lean not on our own understanding but listen to and trust God, He will hear our cry, and we will prevail. In so doing, we will live our God-ordained destiny.

NOTES

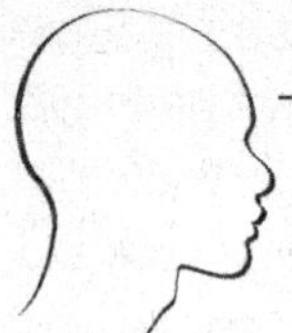

Pardon Me?

By Rev. John Burton Jr.

Lesson Theme	Unit Theme	Scripture
God Forgives	God Is Faithful	Numbers 14:10-20

INTRODUCTION

"Pardon me?" This two-word question is a very familiar statement when someone is seeking to clarify what someone has previously said or done. Additionally, "pardon me" can be used as an apology for whatever was said or done that was not intended. The offense is the key theme in the narrative. If this were a court, the involved parties included: Moses, Aaron, Joshua, Caleb, the Israelites, and God. All parties involved had taken offense by something said or done by the other and felt their points were valid. Feelings were hurt. Emotions ran high. Each had their own way of how to handle the matter at hand, including God. Still, some specific action needed to take place to bring about resolve to prevent further ruin. Although this isn't a tale of hypersensitive people, it can offer guidance on what to do in times of conflict.

MESSAGE POINTS

Message Point 1: "When God Was Offended" (Numbers 14:10–12)

Being called the wrong name, misidentifying someone's age, poor table manners, failing to make an introduction, not picking up after the dog, and many more are things that offend people. Depending on your viewpoint, you may or may not think the offense is warranted. Still, offenses are part of life, whether warranted or unwarranted. However, one thing remains true: someone was offended by it. The Israelites, having grown indignant with the leadership of Moses and Aaron and the reasoning of Joshua and Caleb, were considering stoning them because they were led to a perilous place, the desert. Then God stepped in. He was offended by Israel's blatant contempt. In His anger, He growled to Moses, "How long?" He could no longer allow the furtherance of their disrespect and distrust of Him. God had grown tired of demonstrating His power and provision and Israel remaining defiant and undisciplined. God felt they had abused His goodness and grace, and He was ready to destroy them as a remedy. Amid Israelite complaint and criticism of how they would've faired better dying in Egypt or the desert, God was willing to grant them their foolish request in Paran. He was ready to strike them down with a plague, like those they had witnessed in Egypt.

Message Point 2: "When Moses Interceded" (vv. 13-19)

Every now and then, each of us needs to refresh our memory. God, in all of this rage, was provided that from Moses. In an attempt to defuse the Lord's anger, Moses provides God with a fresh perspective. He sought to remind God of His reputation, not with the children of Israel, but with the Egyptians. Moses alerted God that the Egyptians would talk gossip and gloat, not as a showcase of His justice but as a weakening of His power. Although He performed mighty works on their behalf before—seeing them face-to-face, being a cloud by day and a pillar of fire by night—the resounding statement would be not of His greatness but of His inability to keep His oath to them by allowing them to enter the Promised Land. Moses would bring His own characteristics to mind: slow to anger, abounding in love, always willing to forgive sin and rebellion, but still strong enough to not leave the guilty unpunished. After providing an unofficial deposition, Moses simply implores God because of His great love to do one thing: "Forgive them." It would be a divine demonstration of His mercy.

Message Point 3: "How God Pardoned" (v. 20)

As anxious as a lawyer working on a landmark trial awaiting a jury's verdict, I'm sure Moses waited with bated breath for God's response. He probably wondered, "Was I compelling enough? Would God be merciful just once more?" Suddenly God rendered His verdict: "I have pardoned according to thy word." Moses' prayer of intercession saved an entire nation from destruction. The severity of their deserved punishment was curtailed. God's ability to hear his pleas should be a great source of encouragement for intercessors and others. Moses' effectual and fervent prayer saved Israel from ruin. Although it did not remove the consequences of their sin, God still offered forgiveness. The Israelites' restoration did not mean they would receive all of what was promised, but they still received more than what they truly deserved, death. One sincere prayer saved a multitude. How is your prayer life?

THAT'LL PREACH

In 2007, shots rang out in a one-room Amish school. Ten innocent children were killed execution-style by a gunman, who later killed himself. The families of the victims were devastated! Yet within hours, the Amish community forgave the shooter. Before the blood of the children dried, members of the community were knocking on the door of the home of the gunman to visit his wife. They brought gifts of food, flowers, and extended hugs to members of his family that were present. Though it was stated that very few words were spoken, the presence of forgiveness and grace spoke louder than words. When most would feel the right to be angry, hold a grudge, and be offended, the Amish community chose to forgive and extend grace. Days later at the gunman's funeral, half of those in attendance were the Amish community. Ironically, many had just buried their slain children a day before. If that wasn't enough, the same community contributed money to the gunman's family. Most people cannot fathom that level of forgiveness! For most people, forgiveness takes time, sometimes even years. One father who lost a daughter in the shooting declared, "Forgiveness means giving up the right to revenge." For the Amish, forgiving is a faith requirement! What an example of how God is so quick to forgive us for our sin.

CONCLUSION

Forgiveness for an offense is not always granted. Some crimes and sins come with accompanying punishments for the offense. When we feel offended by someone else, we sometimes withdraw from the person. While the world says we are justified by our actions, God calls us to be different. Like the Amish community reminds us, God asks us to forgive. He says forgive seventy times seven times (Matthew 18:22). Why? Because God is always willing to forgive us.

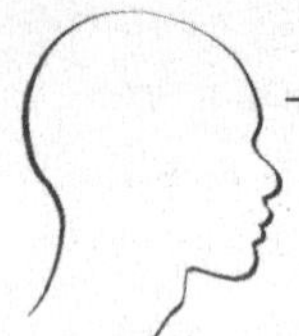

Growing Pains

By Rev. Jaimie D. Crumley, MDiv

Lesson Theme	Unit Theme	Scripture
Obedient Faith	Responses to God's Faithfulness	Deuteronomy 4:1–8, 12–13

INTRODUCTION

In today's Scripture, we meet Moses near the end of his leadership over the Israelites. Having led the Children of Israel through the wilderness for nearly forty years, his journey with them is almost over, and in this passage, he clarifies the laws of the Lord. Moses cannot continue to serve as the moral leader of the group; it is time for the Children of Israel to follow God of their own volition. Obedience can sometimes seem remedial, but this Scripture elucidates the fact that obedience is a sign of maturity. Like a parent or guardian who is preparing a child for the transition from adolescence to adulthood, Moses teaches the Israelites to be faithful and to teach future generations to live faithfully. As the Apostle Paul told the Corinthian church (1 Corinthians 13:11), it is time for the Children of Israel to put away childish things and to mature into the people (and the community of faith) God is calling them to be. Moses frames his command using the language of consequences; those who follow God will live, and those who do not face certain death.

MESSAGE POINTS

Message Point 1: "Staying Alive" (Deuteronomy 4:1–4)

We will not survive our wilderness experiences, and we cannot achieve the magnificent plans God has for us if we do not faithfully follow God's laws. Have you ever had a wilderness experience like the Israelites? To survive wilderness experiences, we need three things. First, we need support from others; second, we need sustenance for the journey; and third, we need unshakable faith. In Deuteronomy 4:1–4, Moses demands obedience to the laws of God. He issues this command while the Children of Israel continue to live in a spiritual and physical desert. Without the grounding of the loving and all-powerful God who was with their ancestors and will be with them for generations to come (support from others), the Israelites cannot complete their journey. Without the laws of God (their sustenance), the Israelites cannot enter and occupy the land God is giving them. Without believing and closely following the law (their faith), the Israelites literally cannot live.

Message Point 2: "Shine the Light" (vv. 5–8)

The Children of Israel are to remember and abide by these laws. They are to follow the laws not just because they know God has been faithful to them, but also so that the other nations will know how faithful God is. They have come this far because God has cared for them, led them, and quite literally kept them alive, and their faithfulness to God's law ensures that they and future generations will continue to be witnesses to other nations of God's goodness. They are to live in such a way that it is obvious to everyone around—even if they don't know anything else about the Israelites—that the Israelite's God is wiser and nearer than any other god they could think of.

Message Point 3: "Honor the Covenant" (vv. 11–13)

God has been faithful to the covenant He made with the Children of Israel, and it is their job to be faithful by obeying God's laws. God is committed to making His relationship with Israel work. In Deuteronomy 4:11–13, Moses reminds the Children of Israel of the commitment that God made to them at Horeb. Because God made this commitment with them and has honored it, they have survived their journey. He reminds them that although they were afraid as they saw God speak to them from the fire, God had spoken to them directly. Because of God's continual faithfulness to them, Moses challenges the Israelites to honor their covenant with God by following God's laws.

THAT'LL PREACH

In the 1994 animated Disney feature film *The Lion King*, a young Simba has lost his father. He runs away because he fears for his life. However, with time he becomes less fearful of losing his life and more fearful of the depth of the responsibility that comes with being king. One night his father appears to him to remind him of the value of his life and to encourage him saying, "Remember who you are; you are my son." In the same way, Moses' constant demands to the Children of Israel to follow God's commandments is an exhortation to them that they must remember who they are. They are not a group of aimless nomads wandering in the desert. They belong to God and belonging to God comes with a set of important responsibilities.

CONCLUSION

God will lead us through the most challenging moments of our lives, but we are required to lean on each other, to have faith, and to follow the commands of God. Although obedience can sometimes seem remedial, following the commands of God is a sign of maturity. For the good of ourselves and for future generations of the faithful, we must follow God's commands.

NOTES

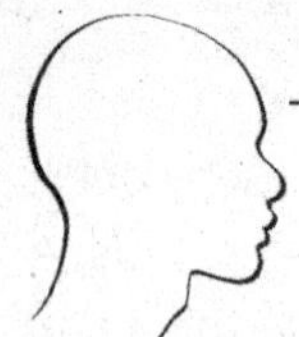

Faithfulness Rewarded

By Kathy Williamson

Lesson Theme	Unit Theme	Scripture
Blessed for Faithfulness	Responses to God's Faithfulness	1 Kings 17:8–16

INTRODUCTION

Have you ever encountered a homeless beggar in front of a supermarket or coffee shop? Individuals holding signs, stating "Will Work for Food," "Haven't Eaten in Days" or simply "I'm Hungry." Sometimes we have offered spare change, feeling good that we were a blessing to someone. Maybe we have donated clothes to a bin or visited someone in the hospital and we're left feeling as though we were a part of God's divine plan to help the poor, the sick, and the needy. Can you imagine if, on the contrary, the recipient of the blessing could quite possibly be you?

MESSAGE POINTS

Message Point 1: "The Brook Dried Up" (1 Kings 17:8–9)

Elijah, having heard from God, declared that there would be neither dew nor rain in the next few years. Even with this declaration, Elijah was unable to make preparation to sustain himself. God instructed Elijah on where to go, making provisions along the way. Elijah did according to the Word of the Lord and as promised, God made provisions for him along the way. Sometime later, the brook dried up. There are times in our lives where the brook simply dries up. The need is greater than our visible resources. And even in this state, we are called to faithfulness and trusting the Source. Again Elijah was given instructions from God. He wasn't sent to someone with abundance. Elijah was sent to a widow woman, someone whose need was greater than his own.

Message Point 2: "A Challenged Faith" (vv. 10–12)

As followers of Christ, we are called to faithfulness. Our faithfulness is believing the word of God even in challenging times. It is a natural response to survey our own resources prior to blessing others. We are challenged to give, even in our lack, and to trust God, often even when we don't see how the story will end. It is not likely that Elijah or the widow woman understood the plan of God. But what they did know is that their faith in the word of God was sufficient. In an effort to see if this was the widow woman to whom he was sent, Elijah asked her to bring him a vessel of water. As the woman went to comply, Elijah took it one step further, asking that she also bring him food to eat. Recognizing that Elijah was a man of God, the woman responded to his request with, "As the LORD thy God liveth, I have not a cake, but an handful of meal in a barrel, and a little oil in a cruse: and, behold, I am gathering two sticks, that I may go in and dress it for me and my son, that we may eat it, and die" (v. 12). In her mind, the amount she had wasn't sufficient for herself and her son, yet she recognizes that she is called to share even that portion. It is not necessarily a sacrifice when we give out of our abundance. It is a challenged faith that calls us to give when we can no longer see our own way.

Message Point 3: "A Faithful Reward" (vv. 13–16)

When we trust God, His faithfulness is revealed. Our obedience to care for others, to become the extension of who God is on earth, will always lend a faithful reward. We don't bless others seeking a blessing in return. In our faithfulness to our call, even in small moments, we see the active hand of God in our lives. Elijah tells the woman, "Fear not; go and do as thou hast said: but make me thereof a little cake first, and bring it unto me, and after make for thee and for thy son. For thus saith the LORD God of Israel, The barrel of meal shall not waste, neither shall the cruse of oil fail" (vv. 13–14). Because of her obedience and faithfulness, God's promise was revealed in her life. She, her son, and the man of God did eat for many days. We don't always see the evidence of God's hand in advance, but we are confident in knowing that in our lives, God is always masterfully orchestrating the plans for our lives.

THAT'LL PREACH

A colleague of mine shared a story of her time at a Memory Care Center where she leads worship for the elderly. Following worship, she decided to sit between two elderly people on a couch listening to the musicians play the closing songs. As she sat between the two, intending to have an adult conversation, she sunk into the couch with her feet dangling off the edge. Immediately, the 103-year-old woman to her right gently took the throw pillow from behind her back for support and placed it behind my colleague's back. The woman then whispered, "It's okay that you're small, I'll help you." At that moment, while she believed she was sent to bring joy and hope to someone else, she admittedly realized the joy and hope she was afforded by that one simple gesture. In an effort to adhere to what we believe we are called to do as believers in Christ, we give of our time, resources and sometimes, even out of our lack. It is in those moments of faithfulness that we provide God an opportunity to fulfill His promise that our flour will not run out nor our jug of oil fail because God rewards faithfulness.

CONCLUSION

Not unlike the widow women, we are often reminded of our own needs. As she looked at her jar of flour and jug of oil, we too look in our bank accounts and grocery stores. It is in those moments we are afforded an opportunity to become a part of God's great plan. It is in those moments that God could be utilizing our circumstances to meet our needs. As faithful believers ,we confidently rely on God, trusting that He will supply all of our needs. And our needs are often met out of our faithfulness to others.

NOTES

____

____

____

____

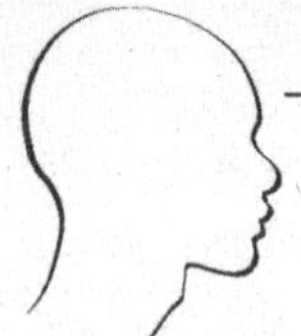

Faith Can Heal

By Wayne Hopkins

Lesson Theme	Unit Theme	Scripture
Faith Can Heal	Responses to God's Faithfulness	Luke 7:1–10

INTRODUCTION

Faith is something we tend to take for granted until we have to use it. Much like searching the hoard of clothing in our closets for the perfect garment or raiding the stash of goods in our pantries for the exact ingredient, we consider ourselves abundant in faith until it is tested and we are not quite sure what to do. The good thing about faith is that it can perform multiple tasks simultaneously. Faith can at once bring calmness and confidence. It can encourage and exhort. It can inspire and ignite. Yet even with faith, there are times when it's hard to find faith to bring into action. This is difficult particularly when it comes to illness. But faith is the physician that needs no tools; it is the specialist for every patient. Faith needs neither pill nor potion to prove its power.

MESSAGE POINTS

Message Point 1: "Faith Doesn't Discriminate" (Luke 7:1–4)

A centurion, a servant, and the Jews: these classifications of people represent the diverse potential of Christianity, but they did not yet constitute the body of Christ. The servant's illness has motivated the centurion to seek Christ, but social stratifications almost prevent the connection. How often do we restrict our faith to only work in certain channels? How difficult do we make things for which God has already paved the way? The fact that the servant had accepted his impending death can represent the hopelessness of those who are unsaved. Both good and bad people get sick, but regardless of the illness, those without hope suffer the most in anticipation of death. The Jews eagerly deem the centurion "worthy" (Gk. *axios*, **OX-ee-oce**), meaning he was deserving of Jesus' intervention. The Jews eagerly vouched for their patron's service to the community, something Jesus would surely appreciate, or so they thought. The centurion was a political figure, and similar to modern civil servants, he demonstrated community service by paying for the synagogue and perhaps providing other charitable gifts. This is fine for winning votes, but it does nothing for the soul. The centurion was hedging his bets by asking the Jews' help, but neither his wealth nor his fair-weather friends could give him what he needed. It was his tiny bit of faith. Faith did not care whom he commanded or what he owned or who deemed him worthy. Jesus could recognize his genuine humility, which made him equal to the dying man. They both were in need of the power of God.

Message Point 2: "Faith Doesn't Delay" (vv. 6–7)

A popular go-to Scripture is "Jesus wept," but here, "Jesus went," and that is a most appropriate thing to recall where faith is concerned. We should not rely solely on our understanding of Jesus' inherent deity when considering how quickly He moved toward the centurion's dilemma. It goes without saying that Jesus knew him, knew the servant by name, knew the name of the illness, and all the other factors that would contribute to this situation. What is more important however is that the centurion had no direct connection with Jesus, yet he believed! Romans 10:17 is invoked here as "faith cometh by hearing, and hearing by the word of God." Just as the centurion had heard about Jesus, in turn, Jesus had heard his anguish over the servant. He had heard the servant's suffering. He even heard the Jews' appeal for help. None of these folks had perfect words of prescribed prayer. None of them had studied or labored either in word or spirit, yet they were all channels for faith to move swiftly to Jesus. What do we do when it seems our faith is delayed? We believe but continue to suffer. We trust God, yet we do not have evidence that He has heard or is even interested in answering our prayers. We can rest assured however that faith is not limited by our doubts. It is not delayed by the depth of our dilemmas. The centurion heard about Jesus and believed. His hesitation to encounter Jesus was a sign of respect, but actually worked to expedite the perfect work of faith in God! By allowing Jesus to work in His own way—just by being himself—the unseen became evident, and the substance of God's healing power became evident immediately.

Message Point 3: "Faith Never Fails" (vv. 9–10)

Where do we misplace our faith? What are the stumbling blocks that we set while attempting to help God out, when the last thing He needs is our help? In this miraculous account we do not see laying of hands. We do not hear proclamations or incantations. The centurion's servant is healed simply by the will of God. This is why we must pray without giving God instructions. Rather, we should give God credit for knowing what we need and how to satisfy our situations. Jesus' reaction demonstrates His ability to recognize and utilize irony. The centurion after all, and presumably his servant are both Gentiles! While the Pharisees and other children of Israel sought every possible way to discredit Jesus and those who believed in him, here are two non-believers who are exercising the full power of faith, and Jesus makes it known how ridiculous this is. God has every right to expect a degree of faith from believers, yet we tend to exercise it most when things are going well. Even if we try to be faithful during times of distress, we must remember that it only requires the smallest amount of faith (Matthew 17:20) to invoke the full and undiluted power of God!

THAT'LL PREACH

It's good to know when your faith has friends. Just as the servant probably could not understand or explain his miraculous recovery, he was blessed because his employer had invoked healing faith in Jesus! There once was a talented musician who was dedicated to the church but often absent due to higher paying gigs, often on the road with famous artists. On one of his visits to the home church, he could not understand the sermon, but afterward, he found himself walking to the altar and answering the pastor's invitation to discipleship. The young man understood the uproar at his leaving his musician's post, but could not understand why the pastor and most of the congregation were suddenly overcome with praise and emotion. When the pastor gathered himself, he said, "Son, we have been praying that all our musicians would become members of the church. While you were away, every one of them did, but you were gone. Yet we kept praying, now you are here, and God has answered our prayer!"

CONCLUSION

There is no doubt that faith requires a stretch. The centurion reached beyond his authority into a realm where he had zero control. All he could do was rely on the name and power of Jesus Christ. Little did he know that his act of faith would not only save the life of his servant, but undoubtedly lead countless others to believe, thus saving their lives for eternity. Faith does not discriminate against the high or low. Faith is not slow, even when it seems to hesitate according to our schedules. We serve an eternal God with power unlimited by time, and it is never too late to begin trusting him. Finally, even if our faith is shaken, our least effort to reach out to God is guaranteed to generate a response. God will answer prayer!

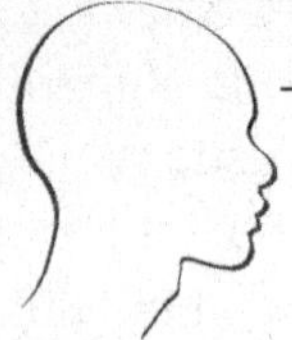

Faith Saves

By Wayne Hopkins

Lesson Theme	Unit Theme	Scripture
Faith Saves	Responses to God's Faithfulness	Luke 7:37–48

INTRODUCTION

The problem with salvation is that it is available to everyone. It is not the world that finds this problematic, but most often those in the church who do. Generations of church culture and practice have shifted the focus away from simple biblical truths and toward rigid conformity, meaning it has become more important to be accepted than to become saved. Once again Luke shows Jesus actively removing barriers between social classes, religious elite, and even attitudes toward women. He makes it clear that despite the road we take to get to Jesus, once we have encountered him, He alone is the way.

MESSAGE POINTS

Message Point 1: "The Fear of a Sinner" (Luke 7:37–38)

This woman knew her reputation, both the parts that were accurate and those that were manufactured by local gossip. One of the most effective tools of sin is when it traps us in fear of the opinion of others. It could very well be that despite her own reduced stature in the community, the Pharisees were similarly subject to disdain from those whom they may have ridiculed or held to impossible standards in the name of the Law. She undoubtedly had occupied her "proper" place on the fringes, and in doing so may have been able to observe Jesus expertly deflecting the Pharisees' accusations. Upon hearing that Jesus was to dine at the Pharisee's home, she may have thought it more than an opportunity to make a desperate appeal. She may have knowingly risked her own life simply to show solidarity with this man who had given life, hope, and opportunity to those who previously had nothing. The woman came in weeping, demonstrated her commitment by wiping Jesus' feet, and provides an awesome example of working through one's challenges in order to exercise trust in God. Perhaps she recalled the words of Psalm 34:4: "I sought the LORD, and he heard me, and delivered me from all my fears."

Message Point 2: "The Fault of a Saint" (vv. 39-43)

The hosting Pharisee takes a great risk in offering hospitality to Jesus. Now, this nameless yet infamous woman puts the Pharisee beside himself with fear and agitation. He makes her sin a spectacle, but it is not the woman's sin, it is the Pharisee's, that is the most harmful here. He judges this woman and goes further to criticize Christ for not rebuking her. Jesus recognizes the fault in the man's reaction and explains that everybody—even the Pharisee—is at the mercy of a loving God. Rather than spew platitudes at the woman for her impudence, his focus should be on gratitude to God for visiting him in his home and forgiving him of his sins. It is easy to look down and lay blame upon others, but the tougher and greater task is to keep an open mind that may lead someone to God.

Message Point 3: "A Faith that Saves" (vv. 44–48)

Undoubtedly the Pharisee credited himself as being an example of humility and hospitality by inviting Jesus into his home, but he still had yet to invite Him into his heart. As Jesus used the parable of the debtors he undoubtedly helped the Pharisee to realize how he may have harmed or disillusioned others with his arrogance. While we should not turn a blind eye to sin, we should neither turn our backs upon the sinner. Deuteronomy 10:12 encourages us to love and serve the Lord, which is what He requires, and this is precisely what this woman had the courage to do. Jesus poked holes in the man's gestures and demonstrated how the woman was actually adding value to his meal beyond his rich provisions. Her bold step to enter without escort, without invitation, and without shame, demonstrated how true repentance shows respect to God and provides restoration to those who dare to believe.

THAT'LL PREACH

Jean once visited the church where her friend Kelli was a member. Jean noticed a woman come in, looking like she had slept in the gutter. She participated in the service loudly. Even with the saints in worship, her voice stood out. Her claps were violently loud, and each "hallelujah" sounded as excruciating as it was exuberant. Jean asked her friend, "Is she a member?" "No, girl, Corrine just comes and disrupts the service every time she gets loaded. She may not even remember where she is when the service is over." Yet, when the pastor gave the invitation, Corrine came to the altar, fell on her knees, and continued to shout, "God, forgive me. Lord, I'm sorry." The pastor explained that God had sent Corrine to shout for someone in the church who was being silent. He prayed that anyone fighting addiction, depression, or abuse would be delivered. Then, one by one, folks shed their shame and came with Corrine, humbly before a loving, forgiving, saving God.

CONCLUSION

No one is perfect except Christ. However, we are called to strive for the perfection or completeness that can only be found in Him. Rather than having faith in a salvation that can be bought or earned, better to seek the one freely given and maintained by God's amazing grace.

NOTES

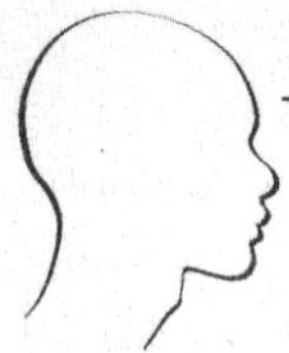

Put Your Things in Order

By Rev. Jaimie D. Crumley, MDiv, STM

Lesson Theme	Unit Theme	Scripture
Self-Examination	Faith Leads to Holy Living	2 Corinthians 13:1–11

INTRODUCTION

When was the last time you were thoroughly inspected? Maybe your inspection happened during a yearly checkup with the doctor who has told you that this is the year you must get serious about taking care of your health. Maybe your inspection happened when a close friend pulled you aside to discuss some recent tension between the two of you. Maybe your inspection happened during an annual evaluation at work when you learned whether you were being considered for a raise or promotion. We all face milestones in our lives that force us to own up to how we have performed physically, interpersonally, or professionally. In 2 Corinthians, the Apostle Paul performs a spiritual inspection on the members of the church at Corinth. Unlike the annual physical exam or an evaluation by a supervisor, a spiritual inspection requires you to self-examine because Jesus Christ is meant to reside within us.

MESSAGE POINTS

Message Point 1: "Finding the Power Within" (2 Corinthians 13:1–4)

We are weak without the power of Jesus Christ. Our weakness is part of the human condition, but as believers in Jesus Christ, we find the power to do the work God has called us to do in the world. Paul warns the members of the church at Corinth that this will be his third visit to them. Although he was lenient with them on the previous two visits, Paul warns that on his third visit, he will discipline those who continue to walk in ways that are inconsistent with God's call on their lives. He knows that those who continue to sin can improve their behavior. Although they are weak by themselves, Jesus is strong within them. His proof of this point is that it was Jesus' human weakness that allowed Him to be crucified, but it was His divinity that allowed His resurrection. Likewise, although our human flesh is weak, through the power of Jesus Christ, we will be able to overcome every temptation.

Message Point 2: "Test Yourselves" (vv. 5–10)

When Paul arrives at Corinth, he wants to have a pleasant and uplifting visit with the members of the church, yet in this passage, he continues to warn the church about his upcoming visit. He warns that during his visit he will examine their spiritual fitness. He does not want them to be surprised or unaware when he arrives. So, he advises them to examine themselves so that when he arrives they will be found to be without fault. Paul tells them that he and his associates rejoice in the strength of the church. Paul provides this much preamble before his visit because he wants to use the authority God has given him for building up rather than tearing down. Through the discerning power of the Holy Spirit, we can be clear on whether our actions are sinful or if they are holy. Because Jesus Christ lives within us, we have the ideal measuring stick to discern the spiritual quality of the decisions we make.

Message Point 3: "Receive This Blessing" (v. 11)

The idea of sin is pervasive throughout all of the Scriptures. So, a message like the one Paul wrote to the church at Corinth can be frightening or intimidating, but for people who are filled with the Holy Spirit and remain in communion with each other, it is possible to strive toward perfection or sanctification. As Paul concludes this letter to the church at Corinth, he leaves them with a benediction. He chooses not to conclude his letter to them with words of warning but rather with words filled with grace, peace, and compassion. After advising them to put things in order, he encourages them by reminding them to agree with each other and to live in peace. For people who were filled with the power of Jesus Christ, such a benediction is apt as Jesus taught His disciples that the first and greatest Commandment was to love God and that the second Commandment was to love their neighbors as themselves.

THAT'LL PREACH

Everyone who has ever been a teacher knows that a major challenge is helping students prepare for their final exams. Students often request study guides and additional assistance outside of the classroom. Sometimes they even stop lectures and class discussions to clarify what will be covered on the exam and what will not. Sometimes a shrewd teacher encourages students to form study groups to learn from each other's successes and failures over the course of the term. This is the kind of work Paul encourages the church to do in our passage for today. They are encouraged to stop looking outside themselves for assistance and instead to turn to the power of Jesus within them and to the presence of the Holy Spirit among them and to prepare together for their spiritual examination.

CONCLUSION

You will be tested. For better or for worse, being tested is part of our spiritual walk. However, those who embrace the power of Jesus Christ within them will not falter. We must examine ourselves to know that we are ready for any test that might come our way. Most of all, we must be people of grace and peace. It is our responsibility to care not only for ourselves but for the entire community of the faithful.

NOTES

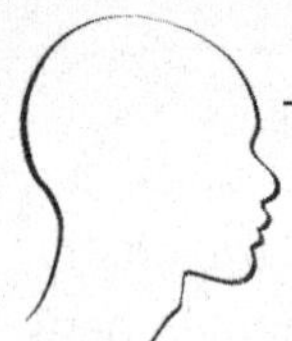

The Balanced Life

By Jerome Gay

Lesson Theme	Unit Theme	Scripture
Be an Example of Faith	Faith Leads to Holy Living	1 Thessalonians 1:2–10

INTRODUCTION

Life is all about balance. Have you heard that word before? We're encouraged to have a balanced diet, not to eat too much sugar, and stay away from fried foods. Financially, we're encouraged to diversify our portfolios and not invest all of our money in one area so we are balanced investors. We're encouraged to read and not just watch television all the time in order to balance our minds. In other words, we want everyone to have balance, but what is balance, really? Even if we have balance in all of the aforementioned areas, would that be enough for us to feel fulfilled? What if the key to a balanced life had nothing to do with you but rather whom you trusted? Paul will show us a totally different way to view life to achieve balance. He gives us the dynamic duo of faith and action. He wants us to understand that our actions and beliefs are inseparable, and in order to have a balanced life, we must have balanced faith. He does this in his letter to the church at Thessalonica.

MESSAGE POINTS

Message Point 1: "The Balanced Life Starts with an Attitude of Gratitude" (1 Thessalonians 1:2)
Paul is grateful for grace and people. Grace is the gift of God to trust Him for salvation, and peace is the product of the gift of grace. We're given grace and peace daily: grace to cover our sin and peace to keep us from shame and guilt. One of the greatest gifts of grace that God has given us is each other. When was the last time you thanked God for a good friend or a member of the church? People are a gift from God, and Paul was thankful for the gift of the body of Christ. He let them know that they were in his prayers.

Message Point 2: "Four Components of the Balanced Life that Reveal We've been Transformed" (v. 3)

1. Faith in Action—Notice that Paul says, "your work of faith." The Thessalonian believers didn't just talk about their faith; they lived it. It was tangible in how they treated people and their actions. Faith is a verb. It's not enough to simply be vocal about God. If your faith isn't transforming your decisions and direction, then it isn't biblical faith.
2. Labor of Love—Jesus tells us that they will know that we're Christians by our love for one another (John 13:35). It's easy to love those who love you back. It's harder to love someone difficult, but we must remember that we were once those difficult people to love.
3. Spiritual Grind—by this, I mean the ability to handle pressure and not quit; it's perseverance. Paul tells us elsewhere to "not be weary in well doing" (Galatians 6:9).

4. Hope—hope in Christ's character is our motivation to persevere. Our hope isn't in anything or anyone of this world, but it's in Christ alone.

The Gospel can't be just about what you say; it must be coupled with what you do. What Paul is saying is that they believed the Gospel, experienced its power personally and witnessed the power of the Gospel in the lives of others. How is this possible? The Holy Spirit brings the conviction to turn from sin and share the truth even when it's unpopular. You and I are sealed with the Holy Spirit for the day of redemption (Ephesians 1:13–14): We're given the Holy Spirit the moment we trust Christ, and He is the seal of the fact that we've been chosen; He validates our election. Paul gives us some of the mechanics of salvation and the work of the Holy Spirit but being chosen also does something else. He gives us joy in affliction. What is joy in affliction? It's not joy based on your affliction but based on what God accomplishes through your affliction.

Message Point 3: "A Gospel Publicly Proclaimed Must be Publicly Practiced" (vv. 4–10)

The Holy Spirit seals us for salvation, convicts us of our wrongs, gives us boldness and courage, and gives us joy in affliction. An equally important role, though, is that the Holy Spirit makes us authentic advertisers.

Notice that Paul tells the Thessalonians, "ye were ensamples [examples] to all that believe." This doesn't mean that they were perfect, but their walk was marked by authenticity. Have you ever been to a concert and could tell that the person singing had a story? The passion they bring to the stage isn't a performance, but rather it's coming from an authentic experience. That's how Christians are supposed to live: we don't hide our imperfections, nor do we celebrate them, but we are to allow our imperfections to be advertisements of His grace.

THAT'LL PREACH

The last thing addressed in this section is how the Holy Spirit saves us from "the wrath to come." What wrath? The word used here deals with God's displeasure with sin and death and God's eternal judgment of sin. So, there's legal language hinted at here. In our current judicial system, a judge might have to recuse him or herself from a case. If there is any bias or prejudice toward a party or attorney, the judge would have to say, "I cannot try this case fairly." Even though He would certainly be joyful if we devote our lives to Him, God the Judge will bring a judgment of wrath on people who aren't in Him. For those who are in Him, however, they're saved from the eternal judgment of the eternal Judge. Paul says that we Christians have been delivered from that wrath!

CONCLUSION

You and I are guilty of eternal treason against a holy and righteous God who is the eternal Judge set to rule justly on all the unrighteousness you and I are guilty of, but Paul says that we're free from that wrath. Why? Because through the Gospel you're no longer an eternal defendant waiting for your eternal death sentence. Instead, you're now related to the Judge. Why doesn't the eternal Judge have to recuse Himself? Because the Judge's Son endured your eternal death sentence so that you can enjoy eternal life. If that doesn't give you joy, I don't know what will.

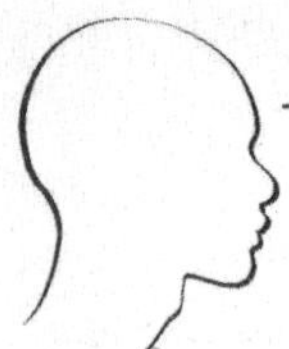

Holiness, That's What I Long For

By Rev. John Burton Jr.

Lesson Theme	Unit Theme	Scripture
Live Holy Lives	Faith Leads to Holy Living	1 Peter 1:13–25

INTRODUCTION

Whenever the word "holy" is uttered, it can conjure up mixed reactions. For some, images of a certain style of dress, nonsecular activities, or all-day worship services come to mind—that is, what's on the outside. For others, it's an upstanding moral behavior, centered on purity in every aspect such as honesty, innocence, and humility—that is, what's on the inside. Too often Christians don't strive for holiness because they consider it an impossible standard to achieve. Why would God request that anyone strive to an unattainable level of perfection? That is a level of perceived difficulty that makes many tend to believe holiness has fallen by the wayside. Many Christians have even sacrificed their holiness in order to try to blend into the culture. In lifestyle, media, and even worship, it is becoming difficult to distinguish sacred and secular. Still, God has an expectation of Christians living holy lives. Is holiness too much of an arduous task?

MESSAGE POINTS

Message Point 1: "Think Differently" (1 Peter 1:13–16)

Does your faith have an effect on the way you live? In a world where Christians are called to stand out, our subconscious goal is to blend in: buying the latest clothes, listening to the hottest songs, and learning the newest dances, simply to be included in culture. There is nothing wrong with culture unless it contradicts your Christian beliefs. For it is written, "Ye shall be holy; for I am holy" (Leviticus 11:44). Holy means to be set apart for God's usage by following His ways. Holiness doesn't begin with what you do. According to Peter, holiness starts in the mind. What you think always determines what you do (Proverbs 23:7). Therefore, he suggests preparing your mind. Entertaining a thought can produce a desire to fulfill the associated action. Think differently! Be "sober-minded," not under the influence of the world and its pleasures. As people born into sin, sinful desires come naturally. It's what you do with the desire that is vital. Clearheaded people know to take sinful thoughts captive and make them obedient to Christ (2 Corinthians 10:5). Christians are converted people living a new lifestyle by letting go of the previous one (Isaiah 43:19). The world's way does not fit; therefore, you must not commit.

Message Point 2: "Bought Differently" (vv. 17–19)

It is said that retail therapy brings pleasure to most people. Going inside a store, selecting an item, purchasing it with cash or a card, and taking possession can be exhilarating. The currency exchange makes the item yours. Christians are God's prized possession! Jesus bought us, not with worldly riches, but with His shed blood. His blood has purchasing power! The value of the dollar fluctuates from market to market. Yet the value of Jesus' redeeming blood remains the same around the world and at any time. God bought you for an expensive price. Therefore, presenting your whole body, physical and spiritual, is a reasonable service to honor God (Romans 12:1). Like the disciples, we are aware of Jesus' amazing sacrifice. This should produce a desire to live holy and not become enslaved by the world and its ways (1 Corinthians 7:23). No money, gold, or silver, would be enough to redeem a soul and save it from everlasting agony. Nothing but the blood of Jesus! Christ's blood saves us from our sins so that we can become holy (Ephesians 1:3–4).

Message Point 3: "Live Differently" (vv. 22–23)

Peter explains the Word of God is a living and enduring word, an imperishable seed (v.23). When planted within a fertile soul, it sprouts a holy lifestyle. The seed, God's word, does not immediately germinate when heard. Only after it's obeyed does spiritual growth occur. When a person responds to the Word and is born again, a new life begins. An inner desire to "want" to live differently should bud. The old idiom goes, "The things I used to do, I don't want to do no more." A new spirit should provide a new perspective. Christians ought to possess a sincere love for their fellow brothers and sisters. This sincerity is not based on any condition but purely on love. At our new birth, Peter suggests, love transforms from less of an adjective (describing) to more of a verb (doing). Expressions of love become not a matter of "I should" but of "I want to." An overwhelming desire is produced because there's a new awareness. The Christ connection makes one want to love their neighbor as themselves, and you are your siblings' keeper (Genesis 4:9, Mark 12:31). This not only pleases others but these expressions of love please God.

THAT'LL PREACH

Contrary to opinion, holy living is not an overnight process. Truthfully, it's not always easy. It's a daily effort that takes time and commitment. Living the world's way is effortless. Its laissez-faire nature suggests doing what you like. Keep in mind, Christians were bought with a price, a high price. Jesus died for you. Why would you want to sell your life so cheaply? You compromise your purchase price by discounting yourself to the world's ways and values. Have a "behind the glass" mentality. In most department stores, the things that are most expensive are kept behind the glass and locked. Only the person with a key can access it when it's ready for purchase. That's where you belong. Holiness is expensive. It will cost you time, effort, and energy. Still, Christ's life costs much more! He came that all could not only have life but more abundant life (John 10:10), not a cheap one. Jesus died for you! Once you fully comprehend His sacrifice, you would understand what your holiness is worth.

CONCLUSION

God created us to be holy. Holiness is not just being separated from sin and secularism. It's the conscious decision one makes to separate themselves to be used by God. It is not a matter of obtaining perfection but a willingness to be perfected for His glory. This sacrifice of surrendering serves as a symbol of gratitude for Jesus' benevolence toward all. Holiness should be our priority, not a preference. A life of selflessness exhibits a million thank yous to God!

When You Know Better, You Do Better

By Allen Reynolds, MDiv

Lesson Theme	Unit Theme	Scripture
Stick to Your Faith	Faith Leads to Holy Living	2 Peter 1:1–15

INTRODUCTION

There is a popular phrase that people use that goes "If you know better, you do better." It usually means that if you have an understanding of how to live and interact in healthier ways, then that's what you do. It's usually meant in contrast to how living in ignorance lends itself to unhealthy behavior. For example if you know eating fried catfish makes your stomach hurt, you stop doing it. If you know you can't go out with your old friend without getting into trouble, you stop hanging out with the person. If you know watching scary movies before bed gives you nightmares, you watch them in the middle of the day. Unfortunately it's not always that simple. Nevertheless, Peter invites us to do better because we know better as believers, and encourages us to help each other do it.

MESSAGE POINTS

Message Point 1: Know What's For You (2 Peter 1:1–4)

Peter starts off by giving greetings, a "What's up?" followed by a "God is good," and a "Hope you're good too, I'm praying for y'all." Then he jumps right into his main point. We need to know what God has promised for us so we can continue to grow in our faith. We are supposed to be living godly lives. What does this mean? We can live the lives God wants for us, full of love, joy, peace, hope, grace, justice, and goodness. We do not have to live lives of worldliness where we don't know how we are going to make it so we fight and backbite to steal scraps from other people. We don't have to be fearful, manipulative, or coercive to get God to take care of us. We don't have to search out the best new philosophy, diet plan, or meditation technique to live right. God has already given us Himself by the power of the Holy Spirit. We have everything we need to thrive. We literally have God living inside of us. God promised to make godly lives happen for us if we have faith in Him and let Him work in us.

Message Point 2: What Do I Do? (vv. 5–11)

After we *know* the promises of God for us in Christ Jesus, we need to work out our faith. Building strong faith takes disciplined workouts. Building our faith is not done by lifting bars or running in place. Adding and practicing the other essentials of godliness strengthens it. Add to faith virtue, to virtue knowledge, to knowledge self-control, to self-control patient endurance, to patient endurance godliness, to godliness brotherly kindness, and to brotherly kindness love. It doesn't improve your daily life to know about Jesus if you don't want to follow His example. Virtue comes before knowledge. You should have the will to do better before you know a bunch of interpretations and revelations. What you know is only useful if you have the desire to use it for good. Then you need self-control because knowing everything means nothing without the wisdom to apply it well. But you have to be patient, consistent in your application if you want your wisdom to flourish because the kingdom doesn't manifest all at once. Then you have to have godliness or god-awareness; otherwise, your patient routines become empty rituals instead of true devotion. And then as passionate as you are, you need to live life with people, other believers specifically, to be a whole believer. We were not called as Christians to serve God in isolation. As you practice this and encourage each other, then you can love everybody the way Jesus called you to in the first place. If you don't practice the process, you are not helping yourself grow as a follower of Jesus. You could become weak and stagnant in your faith, or worse—act like you're blind to God's truth. Instead of practicing godly faith, you would be living life like you don't know better.

Message Point 3: Grace to Act (vv. 12–15)

Peter isn't teaching believers how to do better because he thinks they just don't know better. He knows they know better. They definitely know better than to be out in the world misrepresenting Jesus, acting like they don't know they are saved, pretending that living for God is too hard. The Apostle Peter had the reputation, experience, and authority to remind the believers to know better and do better. There is grace for this life in Christ, even as he received Himself. But we have to use the grace as an opportunily to do better. He knew he would probably be facing death soon, so he wanted to remind everyone to know better and do better. We can remind each other still today; because we know in Jesus Christ, we can live better lives.

THAT'LL PREACH

When I was a kid, whenever we would go out somewhere and my mom wasn't going to be there, I was told to conduct myself in a certain way. And I know my mom wasn't the only one to say this. A lot of my friends heard the same thing. If we were visiting a friend's house, playing an away game, on a field trip, or just outside the house in general, we needed to act like we had some sense. We were told to remember that what we do should reflect well on our parents, our family, our school, and—most of all—our God. We never wanted to be caught doing something foolish and have somebody think, "I wonder who their parents are." We had to act like we were raised better, so we would do better.

CONCLUSION

We have the same call today as people who know Jesus. Jesus raised us from death in sin to abundant life in Christ. When people see us, they shouldn't have to question whether we are a child of the most high God. Here is the key in 2 Peter 1:3. We know better because we know Jesus. It is not what we know that allows us to do better. It is who we know. We have seen godly faith lived out through Jesus, the perfect example. We know Him and are in an intimate relationship with Him by faith. He lives inside of us, empowering us to live faithful and loving lives. We know better. So we must do better.

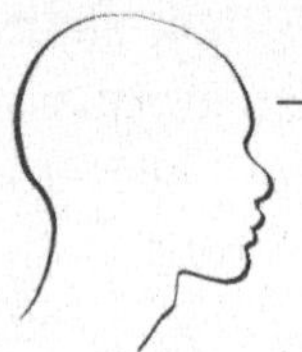

David Worships God in Jerusalem

By Pastor Gabby Cudjoe-Wilkes

Lesson Theme	Unit Theme	Scripture
David Worships God in Jerusalem	David Honors God	1 Chronicles 15:1–3, 14–16, 25–29

INTRODUCTION

The presence of the Lord is something to be cherished. We ought not to take God granting us access to such divine intimacy lightly. In our passage of emphasis, we find that King David has successfully brought the Ark of the Covenant back to Israel. This is a sign of God's favor and God's presence. It is also a sign of how David will lead versus how his predecessor Saul led. As we move through this passage, think about your own leadership style. What is the first thing that you do when you are leading something new? Do you seek out the presence of God? Do you spend time with God? This passage is a powerful case study for all who find themselves facing leadership opportunities in their own lives.

MESSAGE POINTS

Message Point 1: "Who's On Your Team?" (1 Chronicles 15:1–3)

Our text reads that "David said, None ought to carry the ark of God but the Levites: for them hath the LORD chosen to carry the ark of God, and to minister unto him for ever" (v. 2). I find it fascinating that David did not attempt to carry the Ark of the Covenant on his own. Scripture states that it was the Levites whom the Lord had chosen to carry the Ark, but what if David didn't have any Levites on his team? What I find powerful about this passage is that David had a diverse enough team to respond to the demand that the Lord placed on them. Too often, new leaders stack their teams with "yes" people instead of stacking their teams with individuals who will add something to the overall work of the team. I am challenged to push leaders to build a team of people with various skill sets. Some people on your team might even be able to do things that you cannot do. That doesn't make you any less of a leader. Surrounding yourself with people who can meet the needs that you cannot meet on your own actually makes you a wiser leader. Thank God that David had some Levites on his team.

Message Point 2: "Worship is for Everyone" (v. 28)

In this verse, we see that all of Israel is joining in on bringing the Ark of the Covenant home, and everyone is rejoicing with loud shouts and instrumentation. This is a powerful display of David's leadership. David has created an atmosphere where everyone on his team and everyone in his region is worshiping and celebrating the presence of the Lord. A key theological principle here is that we should never take the presence of the Lord for granted. It should be celebrated. People should know what a privilege it is to be visited by God. Furthermore, worship should be demonstrative. No one should be ashamed to worship God. Worship should also be communal. Something powerful happens when everyone worships in one accord.

Message Point 3: "Our Worship Has History" (v. 29)
Verse 29 states, "As the ark of the covenant of the LORD came to the city of David, that Michal, the daughter of Saul looking out at a window saw king David dancing and playing: and she despised him in her heart." As the daughter of Saul, Michal has a relationship to the Ark of the Covenant. She knows how her father engaged with the Ark when he was king. The Ark of the Covenant was captured during the reign of Michal's father, by the Philistines (1 Samuel 6:1). Once returned, the Ark resided in the house of Saul's son, Michal's brother, Abinadab, who was later killed in battle alongside their father. Michal would have known that Abinadab's sons, her nephews, tried to carry the Ark back toward Jerusalem, and that one of those sons, Uzzah, was struck down because he handled the ark directly (2 Samuel 6:6–8). So it's no surprise that by the time the Ark gets to Jerusalem, Michal is less than enthusiastic to see King David rejoicing over its arrival. As Christians, we must be mindful about what we celebrate and how we celebrate it. There is a history that accompanies the highs and lows of our lives. It would be easy to condemn or ridicule Michal, but one must examine her family history with the Ark. We cannot assume that people know why we worship. We must take the time to explain why we do what we do. Not everyone shares the perspectives we share.

THAT'LL PREACH

When a mayor is newly elected to office, he or she must select many officers to serve alongside the mayor's office. One of the most important is the chief of staff. The chief of staff serves as more than just a supervisor of the mayor's other workers. This officeholder should be a mayor's most trusted advisor, who helps make sure the mayor's administration stays on course with the agenda laid out on the campaign trail. By retrieving the Ark of the Covenant, David was named as the Lord's chief of staff. David brought the presence of God back to Jerusalem in a way that would guide their work and protect Jerusalem from harm.

CONCLUSION

King David knew that the Ark of the Covenant belonged in Jerusalem. There will be times in your own life where you are facing new challenges and will be tempted to engage them without the presence and guidance of the Holy Spirit, but do not do so. Let this text be a reminder for you that God desires to walk with you and to advise you on all things. It is fitting for you to give God worship and praise. There is never a time when you are too important or too powerful to worship God fully. But don't stop at your acts of worship; explain to those around you why you worship so that your acts of worship can lead others to Christ.

NOTES

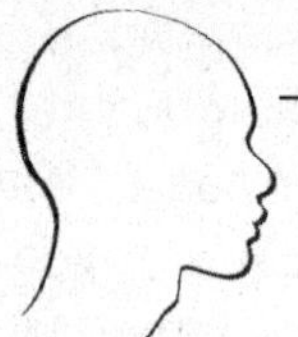

Worship is Real

By Wayne Hopkins

Lesson Theme	Unit Theme	Scripture
A Heart Filled with Gratitude	David Honors God	1 Chronicles 16:8–12, 28–36

INTRODUCTION

Every now and then, a long wait comes to an end. Workers receive their reward, and laborious, fervent prayers are answered. Sometimes we live under a cloud for so long that we forget how the sunshine is supposed to look—let alone feel—and affect our outlook for the better. All too often, Christians allow the conditions of the world to overshadow the things we know and believe above all. How can faith and doubt exist in the same place? That is a basic limitation of the human experience. Our flesh cannot help but focus on the negative. Yet, when God shows up, when the answer comes, when we realize we are not imprisoned by "no" but surrounded by God's overwhelming "yes," then all we can do is give him the praise!

MESSAGE POINTS

Message Point 1: "The Wait is Over" (1 Chronicles 16:8–11)

This passage is preceded by David's triumphal return with the Ark of God and his unbridled celebration of victory (1 Chronicles 16:1–3) during this grand processional, the displays of rejoicing were quite beyond what anyone could label "normal." Sacrifices, cheering, dancing, and a complete lack of shame marked this experience as something never quite seen before—and possibly not since. Surely many of our worship experiences are highly spirited, but not always motivated by the Holy Spirit. Yet when we honestly recognize that God has answered our prayer, defeated our enemy, or simply showed up—that alone is a reason to worship! The phrase "O give thanks" presents thanks as an act not only of gratitude but also of surrender. This indicates that the act of thanksgiving was a bodily effort to show appreciation for God doing what He promised to do. The Bible and our history are no strangers to long waits. It seems that punishment comes quickly and harshly, while the benefits for labor and answers to promises take forever. Yet, when David ushered in the ark, representing the very holy presence of God, he led the people in rejoicing as equals. His kingship was secondary to God's presence as King of kings. Although the wait had been real, it was now done, and praise could truly begin.

Message Point 2: "The Work is Done" (v. 12)

To remember the works of God is to keep a record. In 1 Chronicles 16:4, David instructed the Levites not only to minister and praise, but also, interestingly, to record the proceedings. Imagine that in the days prior to even a printing press, God still had a method by which he would be celebrated as well as remembered. This reveals that our Levitical instruments are not limited to music and song but to the actual documentation and historical preservation of the story of the living God. We must be grateful because God has already done the work we could not do ourselves. David certainly went to war many times, but it was the Lord who fought his battles. The restoration of the Ark would lead to many more activities engaged in by the children of Israel. The building of the Temple was a long way off, yet the holiness of God was celebrated even within the tent. This lets us know that no matter what remains for us to do, we should begin with blessing God for what he has already done. Our gratitude should not be contingent upon what God has done for us "lately." It should begin with knowing who God is and that all things are complete in Him.

Message Point 3: "The Worship Is Real" (vv. 34–36)

To "glory" in praise, presented here in a verbal form, means that praise gets real. The joyful praise reaches its climactic height by loudly proclaiming the goodness of God. Again, the Levites are under David's command to announce and record this victory. Now they are called upon to take a most personal part in this experience, making it a full-body exercise in magnifying God. When worship reaches this level, those looking in from the outside may see it as reckless abandon, perhaps even disrespectful abandon, as did Michal, the daughter of Saul (1 Chronicles 13:29), as she did not understand what she was witnessing. True enough, we often are guilty of evaluating each other's worship under the guise of sincerity. Many denominations codify worship as a currency that must be spent and saved in very particular, peculiar ways. Yet, how can our worship be real if it is bridled by the opinion and permission of others? Has God been good despite who's watching? Has He blessed us without the approval of our neighbors? Did He bless us and bless them too? If God ever deserved our "yes," it is right now in this moment. Giving God glory is not a passive suggestion; it is the bare minimum of what God deserves. It is the very least we can do.

THAT'LL PREACH

A young couple struggled to conceive. Many times they came before the church to announce their pregnancy and ask the church's prayers. Sadly on far too many occasions, they would eventually stop speaking about the new life on the way and grudgingly report that the pregnancy had been lost. The church members meant well and began to burden the young wife with suggestions and remedies to all but guarantee a healthy pregnancy. Through her tears, she would only ask, "Just pray for us." As the couple shared with friends, they realized that they were not alone and that maybe nothing was wrong with them. They decided to put their plans for children on hold and pursue other dreams, primarily travel. After a few weekend road trips, they took a short cruise. The bride experienced seasickness but attributed it to the motion of the waves. Once off the boat, she continued to feel ill and wondered how seasickness could occur on land. A quick visit to the doctor revealed the unexpected truth: she was pregnant. She did not report anything until she began to show, but from the moment she received the news she became a true worshiper. When her child was born she echoed Mary the mother of Jesus and simply said, "My soul MUST magnify the Lord!"

CONCLUSION

Worship cannot be relegated to the sidelines as a necessary annoyance or as a talent showcase for our latest songs and dance steps. True worship begins with a grateful heart. We cannot claim to love the Lord without showing him that love directly, personally, fervently, frequently, and repeatedly. As we pray, remember our wait is over; the hard work is complete. When we acknowledge His awesome works, then our worship is real.

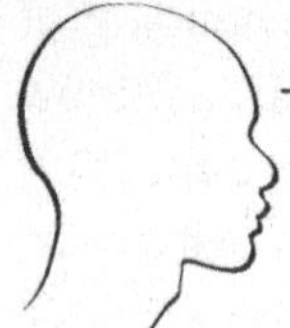

The House That God Built

By Pastor Tommy E. Smith, Jr.

Lesson Theme	Unit Theme	Scripture
Building God's House	David Honors God	1 Chronicles 17:1, 3–4, 11–14; 21:18, 21–27

INTRODUCTION

When Moses gave Israel God's instructions about how they were to worship Him, He included directions for the construction of a portable tent to house the Ark of the Covenant. This tent lent itself to Israel's wanderings in the wilderness but was not intended to permanently house this holiest of shrines. Four centuries later, King David sensed that the time had come to designate a permanent place of worship for Israel's God, the God of all heaven and earth. God appreciated David's desire to honor Him in this way, yet He had His own reasons for denying David this honor. As many of us may know from personal experience, David was not the last person with an unfulfilled desire to do something special for God. As we look back on this incident in his life, we can hopefully receive encouragement from realizing that even though God did not grant David's request, He blessed him in ways David never imagined for himself.

MESSAGE POINTS

Message Point 1: "David's Motivation" (1 Chronicles 17:1)

David's path to sovereignty was not an easy journey. He fought a giant to start with and lived as a fugitive for some time as Saul hunted him in the wilderness areas of the Negev. Finally he had to defect to the Philistines to keep the Israelite forces from trying to apprehend him. There were many times when his life hung in the balance, and he knew that his deliverance from these myriad dangers was solely due to God's provision. So when his battles were finally ended and he found himself surrounded by the luxury of his palace, he wanted God's dwelling place to also reflect the luxurious trappings of royalty. David's desire was the noble intention to bless God in return for His many blessings toward him. He, of course, knew that God was too vast to be contained within any earthly structure, but the desire to show gratitude and thankfulness in a practical way is something that we all should strive to emulate.

Message Point 2: "God's Sovereign Response" (vv. 11–14)

God graciously declined David's offer. Yet His instruction to the prophet Nathan neither reprimands nor chides David for wanting to build a temple for God. Instead, he lets David know that when it comes to offering protection and provision, he is stepping into God's domain. God directed David's thoughts to the important kingly concepts of dynasty and legacy. As Israel's king, David was in a unique position to affect the moral and spiritual life of the nation for a great while to come. This is one of the unique privileges and opportunities of kings, and the Lord identifies this area for special blessings for David. The Lord tells him that He will bless him thoroughly in this regard, and the culmination of these blessings will be that David's own progeny will indeed build God a house, a temple to house His worship, and God, in turn, will establish his throne for evermore! Try as we may, we cannot out-give God!

Message Point 3: "A Spiritually Significant Location" (1 Chronicles 21:18, 21–27)

A temple is a highly symbolic structure. It represents a place where we can commune with God. In Israel's case, the Temple had this significance not only because it was identified as a place to house the Ark of the Covenant, but also because of the Temple's physical location. The temple mount had an interesting and significant history in Israel. Scholars note that the location on Mount Moriah is the same spot where Abraham was instructed to offer Isaac. Scripture also identifies the location as the place where David made intercession to God to end the destruction of the avenging angel who was sent to punish Israel for conducting a prideful military census (2 Chronicles 21:21–27). To commemorate the mercy and compassion God showed by ending the judgment, David was directed to purchase the threshing floor of Ornan (or Araunah) and build an altar. David did so, and this later became the site of the Temple constructed by David's son Solomon. Because of these actions, this place was designated by God as a sacred location. While we have no mandate to build temples today, we can remind ourselves of God's faithfulness by identifying places in our lives as being spiritually significant because of God's intervention and grace.

THAT'LL PREACH

The Crystal Cathedral in Garden Grove, California, is a truly wondrous edifice. Designed by architect Philip Johnson, its name is based on its extensive use of glass for its exterior walls. The 10,000+ glass panels making up its exterior do indeed make it appear as a shimmering crystal in the California sunlight. Of course, not everyone has the opportunity to build or even worship in such a temple. But God has done something even more fantastic! Since the coming of Christ, His Resurrection from the dead, and the gift of the Holy Spirit, our bodies now serve as the temple of the Lord. It is truly wonderful that God has made our bodies now serve as His temple. This means that the opportunity to have intimacy and fellowship, and experience the surpassing power of God's Holy Spirit is available to His followers continually! Building a temple for God is noteworthy, but *being* a temple for God is heavenly!

CONCLUSION

As a man after God's own heart, David wanted to show the world his love and appreciation for God by building Him a grand edifice. As reborn believers and partakers of the divine nature, these same sentiments frequently stir in our own souls as well. Though such aspirations are noble, God does not always allow us to see them to fruition. But God has custom-designed each of us and provided us with life experiences that helped to uniquely define our character. He does this so that we may honor Him in the way He intended. This may not include building a temple, but it does include being a temple!

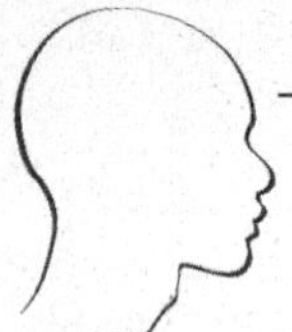

The Lord Is With You

By Rev. Terence K. Leathers, DMin

Lesson Theme	Unit Theme	Scripture
The Lord Is With You	David Honors God	Luke 1:39–56

INTRODUCTION

Luke's Gospel records an encounter between Mary and Elisabeth. They have a commonality that deepens their relationship and allows honest thoughts to be expressed. They both are with child. However, even though they will both have need of nanny services one day, their pregnancies are distinct and different. Elisabeth dealt with the social stigma of being an older married woman who had been unable to have children. Mary's plight is a little different. She is pregnant, but she is unmarried. No doting father-to-be is near. Both women are dealing with societal stigmas. Yet they are able to find the commonality of comfort from each other. These two women are in communion and fellowship with each other.

MESSAGE POINTS

Message Point 1: "Jump for Joy" (Luke 1:39–44)

After Mary's encounter with the angel, she finds her way to Elisabeth's house. As she greets Elisabeth, the baby within Elisabeth responds by leaping. It can be assumed that the baby, John the Baptist, acknowledges the greatness that he encounters and begins to give honor and praise even in his embryonic stage. For those that are babes in Christ and may not be familiar with all of the intricate details of Christianity such as the Apostle's Creed, justification by faith, or any other religious dogma, let me say that more important than any of those things is that you have the enthusiasm and excitement of a child when you are near to and spiritually awakened by the presence of Jesus. The old hymn says "Something got ahold of me," and it later describes that something as the "Holy Ghost."

Message Point 2: "Bless the Spirit" (vv. 44–45)

The Holy Spirit is key to the context and framing of this moment between Mary and Elisabeth. The Holy Spirit allows Elisabeth to speak with a loud voice and bless Mary as she is given the awesome responsibility of being the mother of Jesus. The blessing is not only meant to honor her but it's also meant to remind her that she and the Savior of the world are taken care of in God's sight. Elisabeth's actions ought to remind us that we too have a responsibility to honor and lift our Savior in word and deed. Those who know us ought to have some indication that we have a relationship with Jesus. They should not have to guess which team we are playing for or what banner we will hold.

Message Point 3: "Joyous Praise" (vv. 46–48)

Mary's response to Elisabeth's joy for her is seen in her spirit-filled praise about what God has done for her. It's

Mary's Song of Praise. Mary is visibly happy about God selecting her to give birth to His Son. Her entire body expresses the happiness that God has bestowed on her. Even with the various personal and societal obstacles that may accompany this pregnancy, Mary stands ready to magnify the Lord for what He will do through her and for the world. Here she is, having been associated with the have-nots and the least of these, finding comfort and optimism in what God has selected her to do. One can assume Mary now sees value and self-worth in her very existence. Whenever God comes into your life, He opens the doors of all that you are so that you can view and take possession of your value and self-worth.

THAT'LL PREACH

Isn't it amazing how having contact with someone can clarify purpose and direction for a person's life? When Mary makes contact with Elisabeth, it clarifies her purpose. She knows what she is made for when Elisabeth tells her that she is blessed among women and her child is blessed too. Elisabeth's purpose is also clarified because she finds herself playing the role of an encourager. In Luke 8:26–39, Jesus makes contact with the demoniac. Every time he was put in chains, he would break loose of them and run in the wilderness. But Jesus commands the demons to leave him and enter the pigs. The pigs run down a hillside into a lake and drowned. When people see the man next, he is sitting at the feet of Jesus, aware of all his senses. But this only happens because Jesus makes contact with him and clarifies his purpose and direction. When Jesus makes clear what you were made and designed to do, it not only makes a difference in your life but also in the lives of others.

CONCLUSION

It is evident that after the encounter Mary had with Elisabeth, she felt that the Lord was with her. She knew that God had His hand on her and that the Holy Ghost was guiding and directing her path. As a result, she could praise God even amid the changes in her life. We must remember that God has ahold of us and that He is working everything out for our good and His glory.

NOTES

____

____

____

____

____

____

____

____

____

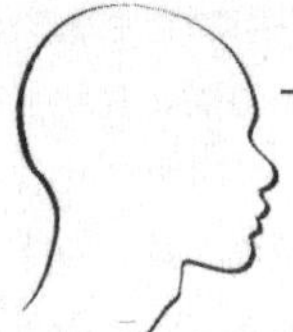

Honoring Up When Shut Down

By Tony Myles

Lesson Theme	Unit Theme	Scripture
David's Prayer	David Honors God	1 Chronicles 17:16–27

INTRODUCTION

Wilbur and Orville Wright are famously credited with inventing and flying the world's first successful airplane. What if before they built and launched it, an authority told them that they wouldn't be allowed to act on their ideas? In fact, extend that hypothetical barricade to other famous inventors, like George Washington Carver, Benjamin Franklin, Thomas Edison, or Garrett Morgan. What if moments before each of them produced their world-changing ideas, they were stopped by a legitimate person in authority telling them to stop? Even more confusing, what if that person didn't explain why at that moment?

It's a tension we all know in the places we work, play, learn, and live. Sometimes we're not allowed to do or make something we're excited to do or make, and what we do next reveals what we're made of. David revealed this when he wanted to build a massive Temple to honor God but was told by the Lord not to proceed. It seems odd until you realize God's much larger plans and perspective (see 1 Chronicles 17:11–12, 22:8). Thankfully, David's worshipful response has much to teach us in how to honor up even after feeling shut down.

MESSAGE POINTS

Message Point 1: "Pocket the Provision" (1 Chronicles 17:16–19)

It's reasonable to acknowledge how unreasonable blessings are. God owes us nothing yet gives us everything: He sets us free from the grip of sin and offers us heaven eternally; He invites us into His mission to save others and provides grace to grow into such a grand purpose; He lets us talk with Him through prayer and speaks to us in Spirit and in truth. And then, on top of all of that, He allows us to experience various perks in life. If you tried to count every one of your blessings, you'd realize how many of them you take for granted.

Perhaps it's why David took the time to "pocket the provision" he'd personally received from God. Instead of being disappointed that he wouldn't build the Temple, David relished in how God had built him and his family into something out of nothing. We can do this too, whether formally through journaling and prayer or simply by pausing during a meal with loved ones and silently thanking God for those we get to do life with. Such gratefulness creates a foundation for worship.

Message Point 2: "Praise the Provider" (vv. 20–22)

Receiving blessings from God doesn't reveal you to be any greater than anyone ever thought but reveals God to be so much greater than anyone ever thought. It's why David paused to not merely thank the Lord for what He'd done but to "praise the Provider" for who He is. What God gives us can help us see Him, and only by seeing Him can we begin to truly see ourselves. For this reason, we must be careful to not turn words of praise into saying the right thing but not having the right perspective. Genuinely praising God for who He genuinely is genuinely resets us; however, giving lip service puts our focus on the religion of Christianity versus the person of Christ. Among the many reasons to praise God, we find that He is ever-present, glorious, powerful, truthful, good, merciful, and more. Those who wisely praise Him will joyfully give credit where credit is due.

Message Point 3: "Pray the Promise" (vv. 23–27)

David considered God's promise as more than enough guarantee to affirm that his son Solomon would also one day serve as king. Perhaps to solidify it in his own heart, David began to "pray the promise." It was his way of not demanding an essay from God that explained everything in the past, present, or future. Instead, David's prayer celebrated how even one word from the mouth of God is enough to live on. God will share the next step when it's time to hear it. Prayer keeps egotism and impatience in check. But a prayer that claims a God-given promise does one more thing—it helps us recognize how God is always among His people. In turn, that reveals that a breakthrough can take place anytime and anywhere if we tune into this reality. We don't need to pray for His presence but for an awareness of His presence. You can pray the promise in your life, whether it's unique to you from God or a promise for everyone that He shares in the Bible. The key is to own it by choice now and by faith into the future. After all, many people know how to routinely pray, but few live dependently on the Lord.

THAT'LL PREACH

"How are you doing?" It's a question we ask each other on a daily basis, although not necessarily something we expect an honest response to. If we actually took the time to share every detail, hurdle, sickness, or trophy in our lives, we'd quickly find ourselves squirming to get out of the very conversation we started. Instead, in our culture, the expected response is, "I'm fine. How are you?" A more accurate reply, however, might be to simply say, "I'm doing better than I deserve." Even on our worst days, we are surrounded by blessings God has given us only by His grace. Perhaps our job offers us benefits, our family inspires laughter, our kitchen contains food, or our toilets flush when we push their levers. Maybe we have a friend or two, know how to read, or live in climate-controlled space. Or, bare bones, you know Jesus died for you and offers you Himself even now. This is the mindset we addressed today through the life of David. It could be that we want something out of life or God we aren't getting. If someone were to ask, "How are you doing?," do you already know the answer?

CONCLUSION

Charles Spurgeon once said, "As long as a man is alive and out of hell, he can't have any cause to complain." David's worshipful attitude in this passage definitely recognizes that framework, for despite leading the Jewish people to the height of their identity in the Lord, he was lowered into humility and accountability. It reminds us to be mindful the next time we're not allowed to bear fruit in something we care about, for we'd do well to root into the Lord instead of pine over ourselves.

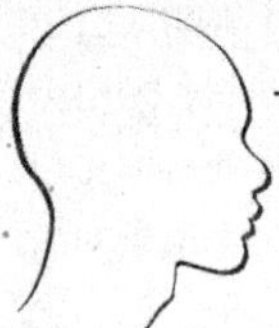

Giving God His Rightful Place

By Ramon Mayo

Lesson Theme	Unit Theme	Scripture
A Place for the Ark	Dedicating the Temple of God	1 Kings 8:1–13

INTRODUCTION

What would you do if a celebrity were coming to your house? I'm sure you would spend time cleaning the place up. You would not spare any expense getting ready for an important VIP to visit your house. You would get the lawn manicured. You would clean things you have never cleaned before. There wouldn't be a speck of dust on any inch of your furniture. You would also probably make sure you had the best food. It wouldn't be Kraft Mac and Cheese or some leftover pizza. You would pull out all the stops in making sure this person felt welcomed and honored. This is what we do for a human VIP. But what about God? He is the ultimate VIP, and He's decided to dwell among us. How do we make our lives ready with a place to honor God, the ultimate VIP? Today I want to talk to you about giving God His rightful place.

MESSAGE POINTS

Message Point 1: "We Need Close Proximity" (1 Kings 8:1–4)

Solomon summoned all the elders of Israel and invited them to escort the Ark of the Covenant from the City of David into the Temple. This was a monumental event. The Ark was where God appeared and was a sign of God's presence. The Temple was the center of religious life and worship in Israel. No longer would God be on the outskirts or just for those in the royal house. Now God was going to dwell in the midst of His people. In order for God to have His rightful place, we can't keep Him at a distance. We need to be close to Him.

Message Point 2: "We Need Right Relationship" (vv. 3–5)

Being close to God all depends on our relationship with Him. The Israelites made a covenant with Him at Mt. Sinai after they left Egypt. The Ark held a reminder of that covenant in the form of the Ten Commandments. God would come and dwell with them because they were His covenant people. And God comes to dwell and live in us because we are His covenant people. Notice that while the Ark was processing through the city, Solomon was offering uncountable sacrifices. The various sacrifices of the sacrificial system offered the Israelites a way to atone for sin and to enjoy fellowship with one another before God. Jesus Christ came to fulfill the sacrificial system, offering us a once-and-for-all offering to make a path to right relationship with God. We need only to examine ourselves and honestly confess our faults to enjoy fellowship with one another before God too.

Message Point 3: "We Need a Proper Response" (5–13)

The priests could not continue their service because of the cloud of God's glory filling the Temple. His presence evoked a response of awe and worship. Solomon's prayer indicates a proper response. His prayer indicates the cry of every believer's heart. We are overwhelmed with awe and worship and yearn for more!

THAT'LL PREACH

If you go near a waterfall, it is likely you will get hit by the spray. You can enjoy the mist as it hovers around you, but you still keep your distance. Some of us choose to treat God in the same way. We enjoy being around God's people or even going to church, but we refuse to be drenched and soaked by the presence of God. That could only happen when we draw near and refuse to keep Him at a distance. Only then can we fully experience the awesome power of the Almighty.

CONCLUSION

Solomon knew it. The priests knew it. The people of Israel knew it. They needed God, and they needed to honor God as God. If you're not honoring God as God, then your life is out of whack. It's off track. When God is in His rightful place on the throne of hearts, then amazing things can happen! Once we have close proximity, right relationship, and a proper response, He can fill our lives with His glory.

NOTES

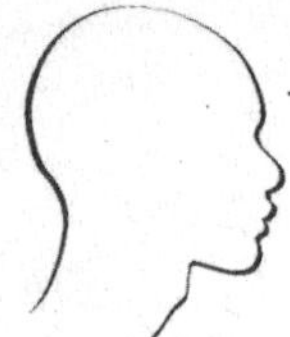

Leaving a Divine Legacy

By Gina A. S. Robinson

Lesson Theme	Unit Theme	Scripture
Solomon's Speech	Dedicating the Temple of God	1 Kings 8:14–21

INTRODUCTION

Do you ever wonder what your legacy will be? What will you leave behind for the generations to come? What imprint will you make on this world? Each one of us is destined to leave a legacy. The decisions we make today will impact the future of our family, church, and community. The prayers we recite daily will be manifested in the lives of those who walk this earth long after we are gone. Our legacy is deeply connected to our relationship with the divine. The type of legacy we leave is dependent upon who dictates our actions. Sometimes we become so focused on doing what we want to do that we never get around to what God is calling us to do. The voice of God is always our voice of reason. We determine which voice is God's through the process of discernment. Discerning God's purpose and plan for our life is key to ensuring God's promise is fulfilled. In today's scriptural lesson, we learn from Solomon how his father David's choice to surrender to God's purpose and be subservient to God's plan resulted in the fulfillment of God's promise during the reign of King Solomon.

MESSAGE POINTS

Message Point 1: "Surrender to God's Purpose" (1 Kings 8:14–16)

Solomon testifies how the dedication of this Temple was destined long before he became king. After Israel had chosen their own king, God chose David to lead the people. In 2 Samuel 7:8–9, we see that the word of the Lord came to Nathan and revealed to him that David would serve as the leader of Israel. David was dedicated to working in a pasture, following sheep, prior to receiving this call from God. Rather than ignoring Nathan, David surrendered to God's purpose for his life. We see how all things worked together for David's good. He went from shepherding sheep to being a shepherd of God's chosen people. God prepared David to lead the people and even promised him a legacy through his son (2 Samuel 7:12–16). Like David, God has chosen each of us to do something special and specific in this world. Our past experiences and present decisions will impact our legacy. The question is: Are you willing to surrender to God's purpose for your life? Stepping out of your comfort zone and into God's will sets your legacy on track to receive God's promise.

Message Point 2: "Be Subservient to God's Plan" (vv. 17–19)

Solomon continues to testify to the fact that David's plan was not God's plan. David considered building a temple or a house for the name of the Lord to dwell. God was pleased with David's thoughtfulness but told him he would not build the house. Instead, this idea would be manifested in the life of his son. Can you imagine coming up with a plan, God-affirming your plan, and then telling you that you are not the person to bring it to completion? Anger, confusion, resentment, or aggravation may be some of our emotions when a plan does not go our way. The text does not tell us how David felt, but we do see by his actions that he submitted to God's plan. We too must submit to God's plan. The idea God gives us might be a seed to plant or pass on for the next generation's growth and development. Everything God gives to us is not for us. We must remember that our legacy is as much of God's plan for our life as our present reality. Being subservient to God's plan sets us up to celebrate the fulfillment of God's promise.

Message Point 3: "Celebrate the Fulfillment of God's Promise" (vv. 20–21)

God upholds His promise in the life of Solomon. He completes this testimony by highlighting his rise to the position of leadership held by his father. God's promise is fulfilled. God chose David so that God could later appoint Solomon to do this great work. This story reminds us that we exist in a continuum that reaches back to the prayers of our ancestors and stretches to the fulfillment of God's promise in the lives of our descendants. We do not have to wait to see what our legacy will be to begin celebrating the fulfillment of God's promise right now. The word of the Lord shows us over and over that the Creator keeps all promises. Solomon built the Temple that was spoken of in the covenant made between God and David, and this is proof that God will fulfill promises in the legacy we leave behind. This story should also reassure us that God's hand is not only on us but also on the next generations connected to us. Take joy today in celebrating the fulfillment of God's promise in the years to come.

THAT'LL PREACH

In her memoir *The Ditchdigger's Daughters,* Yvonne Thornton tells the story of how she and her five sisters became doctors in spite of the racial, economic, and gender-based challenges they faced. Their father had a dream that all six of his African-American daughters would become doctors. He knew that their becoming doctors would change the trajectory of his legacy from poor, blue-collar workers to financially stable leaders in their community. Like David, Thornton's father surrendered to God's purpose for his life. The father worked hard on his job and raised his daughters to focus on the path to becoming doctors. He was also subservient to God's plan. God did not tell him to become a doctor. The dream was to manifest in the life of his daughters. And every one of those women became doctors! Even both of Yvonne's children became doctors. Mr. Thornton's actions and decisions had a direct impact on his legacy. The generational curse of poverty was broken, and God's promise was fulfilled. What must you do today to leave a divine legacy?

CONCLUSION

God is calling each of us to surrender to the purpose assigned to our life. God would not assign us a purpose without providing a plan. We must choose to submit to God's plan if we want to see God's promises fulfilled throughout our legacy. It is never too early to celebrate by thanking God for fulfilling these promises. If God did it in the life of Solomon, then God will do it again in the life of your descendants. These are a few lessons in leaving a divine legacy.

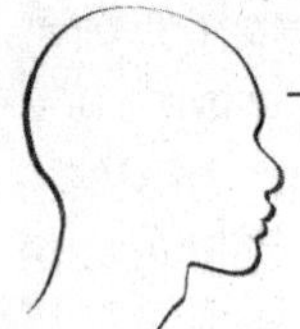

A Grand Opening

By Rev. John Burton Jr.

Lesson Theme	Unit Theme	Scripture
Solomon's Dedication Prayer	Dedicating the Temple of God	1 Kings 8:22–30, 52–53

INTRODUCTION

Red, yellow, and blue helium-filled balloons floated in the breeze. The taut red ribbon with a scalloped bow in the center was secure. Finally, the yellow banner with a slight dimple in the middle and red capitalized lettering reading "Grand Opening" was draped above the front doors. In today's imagery, this array of window plumage signals a celebration is about to occur. Although Solomon wasn't opening a new business, his dedication of the recently completed Temple was just as glitzy. Bronze, gold, and silver decor blanketed the edifice. The guest list was a virtual who's who of those in the area. Among his invited guests were the leaders of Israel, all the heads of the tribes, and the family patriarchs. The Temple's focal piece was the Ark of the Covenant of God, a symbol of God's presence among the people. Solomon wanted all things exquisite for this preeminent celebration and dedication in God's honor. This occasion provided Solomon, as well as onlookers, the ability to witness his earnest thoughts in response to God's goodness in his and his father's lives.

MESSAGE POINTS

Message Point 1: "The Adoration" (1 Kings 8:22–24)

Solomon was grateful for all the Lord had done. His father, David, had desired to build God a temple but was entrenched in war. Therefore, God said no. Solomon was able to build it instead. To express his sincerest gratitude, Solomon wanted to pray and dedicate the Temple himself. It would have been easier for Solomon to request a priest or prophet to perform the task. Yet Solomon didn't want an intercessor; he needed to do it himself. That's how much he wanted God and others to know his deep sense of gratitude for God's kindness in keeping the covenant. Still, Solomon knew the Temple's opulence was more for man than for God. Man looks at the outer, whereas God looks at the heart (1 Samuel 16:7). Therefore in the company of all of Israel, Solomon repositioned himself and spread out his hands toward heaven. Like other activities, prayer involves preparation. He needed to center his mind and spirit to give himself to God first. Solomon changed his posture to reflect one of humility and not superiority. This physical posture was a highly unorthodox act since Solomon was royalty. He wanted to showcase for all, especially God, his deep sense of reverence and thanks. The sincerest gesture is to talk to God in prayer.

Message Point 2: "The Appeal/Affirmation" (vv. 25–30)

After acknowledging God's goodness with Israel and giving thanks, Solomon proceeds to make an appeal. He knew the Temple, no matter how gigantic, was just one place where God could dwell. Still, Solomon hoped this would be a gathering place for God to hear the prayers of Israel and himself. If He could simply hear their petitions, He would continue to extend the grace and favor He promised. Solomon had firsthand knowledge that although God promises, it does not mean absolute possession. Therefore, he pleads, "hearken unto the cry and to the prayer, which thy servant prayeth before thee to day." Solomon is speaking from a place of humility, calling himself a servant. Monarchy is self-directed, and servanthood is selfless-directed. Interestingly, Solomon makes a surprising distinction from this prayer and a previous one. He asks God to pay close attention to his current prayer. There was a level of authenticity attached to this prayer compared to previous ones to make such a distinction. He pleads with God to hear him five times. Solomon asked God to confirm His covenant with Israel by hearing their concerns. If He would just hear them, He would forgive and restore. Solomon knew God's interest in Israel would solidify His involvement in their future.

Message Point 3: "The Attention" (vv. 52–53)

Attention is notice taken of someone or something or the act of taking special care of someone or something. This is what Solomon was asking of God. He requested that God's eyes and ears not only be attentive to his pleas but the pleas of Israel "in all that they call for unto thee." It would seem Solomon had resorted to a posture of royalty and superiority when making such an entitled request. Yet Solomon supplies God with ample evidence that would substantiate his reasoning. He outlines all that God had done in Israel's past: separated them from other nations, made Israel His special inheritance through Moses, and brought them out of Egypt. It would only be in His seeing and hearing that He would be open to hearing their admissions and pleas for forgiveness. Plainly, Solomon wanted God to continue His faithfulness to Israel in their future as He had done in the past. He knew if God was appreciated for His track record with Israel, He would continue to grant them His favor.

THAT'LL PREACH

We are just a few days into the new year. Just a few nights ago, many brought in the new year at a New Year's Eve or a Watch Night service. While inside, you acknowledged God's goodness in the closing year and asked for His blessings in the new. When the clock struck midnight, many celebrated both. In the service, we celebrated corporately and individually what God has done in our lives. Whether you yelled, clapped, danced, or cried, you celebrated the goodness of Jesus. That's exactly what Solomon did. He thanked God for the past and praised Him for his hoped-for bountiful present. Although you celebrated on January 1st at 12 a.m., celebrate again. You have a track record and knowledge of what God has already done with anticipation of what He will do in the future. You don't need a building. You are a living sanctuary, tried and true. Celebrate now! Celebrate again! Because, like Solomon, we know God is faithful!

CONCLUSION

Some things are just worth celebrating—like birthdays, anniversaries, new homes, new jobs, and other major milestones. God's active presence is also praiseworthy. He dwells not only in the heavens but with us, which makes Him never homeless. His presence acknowledges He has not forgotten about His people, still hears their prayers, and keeps His promises regardless of the actions of man. What a reason to celebrate!

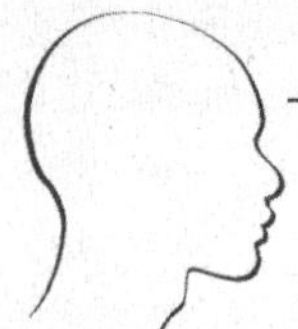

Solomon's Blessing

By Tony Myles

Lesson Theme	Unit Theme	Scripture
Solomon's Blessing	Dedicating the Temple of God	1 Kings 8:54–61

INTRODUCTION

Imagine being asked to run the Nintendo video game company in America, and your last name is Bowser—just like the popular villain who for decades has fought against Mario and Luigi. That actually happened in February of 2019 as Doug Bowser "leveled up" from another position in the company to become the new boss. Being "named appropriately" like this for a job could also include Zoe Hamburger, who worked in field marketing for McDonald's, the lightning-fast Olympic sprinter Usain Bolt, ABC News meteorologist Amy Freeze, English Romantic poet William Wordsworth, and a New York lawyer named Sue Yoo. The question in all of this becomes if your top goal is to make a name for yourself or if you'll elevate the larger name you work for. Solomon faced a similar question in being known as the son of David ("a man after [God's] own heart," Acts 13:22)—as the next king, he could either promote his own name or the name of the Lord. The Temple's dedication was the perfect opportunity for him to clarify where he stood and to help the people properly worship the living God.

MESSAGE POINTS

Message Point 1: "Worship God Personally" (1 Kings 8:54–55)

The text notes that Solomon stood up from kneeling after praying and seeking God with his hands held high, and we must not cheapen the meaning of this by quickly reading over it. It was the typical ambition of a king to establish their name and kingdom, and yet here Israel's human king takes the time to recognize who the true King is. By personally worshiping the Lord on his knees, Solomon gained the footing to stand and lead the people in worship. They were all then called to respond to the One they couldn't see after watching a rich, powerful and successful (yet quite flawed) man they could see honor Him. While no house could contain the Lord, no social status could contain Solomon's worship. For us, it's a reminder that personal worship is not private worship—it's not a retreat from reality, but it is an encounter with God in reality.

Message Point 2: "Worship God Historically" (vv. 56–57)

The very idea and construction of the Temple represented a powerful (and sometimes spotty) history to the Israelites. For centuries, they'd struggled to claim the identity God had given them while not always being faithful to all that God asked of them. Still, the Lord never abandoned them when they abandoned Him, and Solomon recognized this by worshiping the Lord for the past. God was with them when they were living in slavery in Egypt, walking the desert toward the Promised Land, claiming geography for a physical kingdom, and everything in between. This Temple was not merely the exclamation point at the end of that journey but a sign that He would continue to find new ways to dwell among them. All of this is a striking reminder to us to not overlook the Lord's faithfulness. One of the clearest ways to see God in the present is to clearly remember Him in the past. In order to grow, we must tap into our roots.

Message Point 3: "Worship God Futuristically" (vv. 58–61)

Sadly, our nature tries to tame God or stop advancing in our faith; it's easier to learn how to "talk Christian" than to continue confessing our need for Jesus and being transformed by Him each day. Even our desire to have a faith we can tangibly experience, talk about, and understand distracts us from how God is absolutely reliable yet absolutely unpredictable. Solomon calls the people to this tension by daring them to consider the opportunities ahead. Instead of letting everyone be "all right" with this amazing divine experience, he wanted them to *get right* with the Lord so they'd walk with Him in every experience. Even more so, he wanted the whole world to know who the Lord is. If we want to see more spiritual outsiders become spiritual insiders, spiritual insiders need to get outside of themselves.

THAT'LL PREACH

A generation earlier, Solomon's father David was enthusiastic about creating this very Temple that Solomon was credited with building. Instead, God told David then to let what He had done in his life be more than enough. Had David not obeyed the Lord in that, Solomon would have been deprived of his personal defining moment that became a defining moment for the whole people. Like these two men, we can also struggle to make our mark in this world—whether it be for personal gain or spiritual achievement. If we're not careful and mindful, we'll pursue titles and entitlements as benchmarks that we're in step with God. It's important to remember that the Lord desires obedience more than sacrifice and that He allows every person in every generation to choose between the two. We each play a role in each other's journeys, but every one of us stands before God individually. One generation's "ceiling" can become the next generation's "floor" in so many human-sized ways, but only if the Lord builds the house will its laborers not build in vain.

CONCLUSION

Be careful not to confuse building the church with playing church. Let faithfulness and worship be enough, trusting that God is using you in ways you can't yet see so that others can one day see Him. If you want to know for sure that you're doing God's work God's way, pay attention to what's happening in you and others. For example, Israel's worship leader on the day of the Temple dedication wasn't a priest but a human king. That's just not common, although it is what God would consider normal. It's also a stark reminder that Christianity at its core isn't a religion meant to get you into eternity. Rather, it's truth for life so you can meet the truth and life to become a product of the truth beyond life. May our worship be personal, historical, and futuristic. May we determine today who God is calling us to be tomorrow. And may we dedicate ourselves as living temples of the Lord.

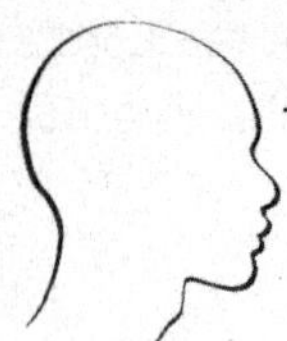

My Desire Is to Please Him

By Ramon Mayo

Lesson Theme	Unit Theme	Scripture
Single-Minded Obedience	Jesus Teaches About True Worship	Matthew 4:1–11

INTRODUCTION

Most people don't have an all-consuming desire. Most live their life influenced by different distractions and obligations. When you see someone who has an all-consuming desire, it's different. They will not stop until they get what they want. They will not turn aside for anything else. Some people call it fanaticism, but as followers of Jesus, we need to take a cue from Him and incorporate His all-consuming desire to please the Father into our lives. The title of my message today is "My Desire Is to Please Him."

MESSAGE POINTS

Message Point 1: "When Your Desire is to Please God, You Will Not Give In To The Cravings Of Your Flesh" (Matthew 4:1–4)

Jesus had been alone in the wilderness fasting for forty days and forty nights. The devil came and attacked His identity and also tempted Him to turn stones into bread. Well, what's wrong with turning stones into bread? It's not about turning stones into bread; the real issue is listening to the devil to satisfy your needs. Jesus rebukes Satan with the Word of God and lets Him know God will supply all His needs.

Message Point 2: "When Your Desire Is To Please God, You Will Not Exalt Yourself" (vv. 5–7)

Jesus is tempted again by Satan. The devil takes Him to the highest Temple and tells Him to jump and show off His spectacular power since God will send angels to catch Him. But Jesus lets him know it's not about Him; it's about God. The enemy wants to trick Jesus into demonstrating pride instead of humble submission. When you truly desire to please God, you don't want to show off. You want to serve.

Message Point 3: "When Your Desire Is To Please God, You Will Not Be Distracted By Good Things" (vv. 8–11)

The last temptation Satan presented to Jesus is to bow down to Satan. Now it wasn't just a direct request to bow down, but Satan asks Jesus to bow down in exchange for the kingdoms of the world. This is what Jesus is after anyway. He wants the world to come to know and worship Him and the Father. It's the right end, but the wrong means. Bowing to Satan is a distraction from the mission God gave Jesus. Christ must fulfill this mission through sacrifice on the Cross. Sometimes we can be distracted by good things and go about getting these good things the wrong way. Eventually, we obtain the good thing but miss out on God's best. A true desire to please God isn't distracted by good things but focuses on God's best.

THAT'LL PREACH

One day a man came to Socrates desiring to learn from him. Socrates led him to a river and asked "What do you want?" and the man said "Knowledge." Socrates proceeded to lower the man under the water and held him down for thirty seconds. Then he asked him what he wanted again, and he responded again, "Knowledge." Socrates then proceeded to dunk the man under the water again. Soon he came up gasping for breath. They went through this one more time until the man came up gasping and crying out, "Air. I want air." We need to desire to please God in the same way this man wanted air. Knowledge is good. Wisdom is good. Bread is good. Trusting God to protect you is good. All the kingdoms of the world belonging to God is good. But living your life driven by a desire to please God—that is the best!

CONCLUSION

Satan attacked Jesus' identity and His mission. He will do the same to us. We need to be secure in who we are and the purpose God has given us. You may not know the specifics, but all believers are called to please God. When your desire is to please Him, then you will be able to resist the lure of temptation. Remain focused in your desire to please Him.

NOTES

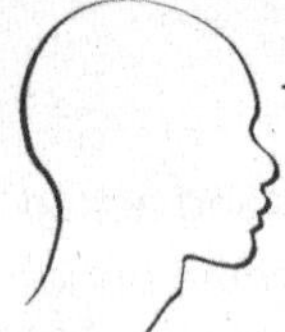

What Not to Do

By Dr. Rev. Matthew C. Jones

Lesson Theme	Unit Theme	Scripture
Piety That Honors God	Jesus Teaches About True Worship	Matthew 6:1–8

INTRODUCTION

In Matthew 6, Jesus gives His disciples a lesson on the good and the bad. Specifically, He talks to them about what to do and what not to do when it comes to our worship and our lives before God. Some of the good things our Lord discusses are almsgiving (Matthew 6:2–4) and prayer (vv. 5–6), but these goods can turn bad when they are done with a look-at-me attitude. Rather than drawing attention to ourselves, true worship draws attention to our Lord, and it flows from living in His mercy and by listening to the Messiah. In this study of the first eight verses, we will see these principles in Jesus' teaching, as He instructs His disciples to embrace the good while exposing the bad that derails our lives and worship.

MESSAGE POINTS

Message Point 1: "Look at Me" (Matthew 6:1–2)

The first verse of Matthew 6 begins with an old rabbinic technique that scholars refer to as a kelal sentence, which means an opening line that contains the themes of the following sentences. The opening words of the verse should grab us. Jesus warns us, "Take heed that ye do not your alms before men, to be seen of them." This is the look-at-me attitude, which is not to mark followers of our Lord. It did, however, mark some of His haters and the spiritual types of Jesus' day (e.g., the Pharisees), who were known for showing off their piety. If they had Instagram or Facebook, these guys would have been posting their almsgiving and prayers for everyone to see and like them. In verse 5, Jesus talks about how they prayed in public to be seen. True worship, on the other hand, makes little of the self, for as we behold ourselves before the holy triune God, we realize our need for mercy.

Message Point 2: "Living in Mercy" (vv. 3–4)

The tone of Jesus' teaching is serious. He begins with a word of warning, which could be translated as "be very careful." Our Lord knows we are prone to wander into places of danger. Because of this, we can make good things like prayer and almsgiving into bad things. In verses 3 and 4, Jesus teaches His disciples a kind of giving and intercession that flows from God's mercy, wherein knowing the Father sees us is all that matters to us. Rather than giving to be seen by others, Jesus directs us to the gaze of His Father. As we stand before God the Father, we realize our need for a Savior. After all, we have not given as we should or prayed as we should (1 Thessalonians 5:17), and (let's be honest) we have done acts of piety to be seen by others. That said, praise be to God, we have Jesus who gave His life for us and perfectly obeyed the law. As we look to God the Son and listen to Him, we find forgiveness and hope of a greater reward that is to come by His mercy.

Message Point 3: "Listen to Messiah" (vv. 5–8)

In verses 5 through 8, the Messiah teaches His disciples about the good of true worship and piety. He describes it as the antithesis of hypocrisy. In fact, Jesus calls out the "hypocrites" (v. 5), which was a term in Jesus' day used for actors. Jesus is indicting the empty spirituality as practicing a show-time religion; that is, they were praying and giving just to put on a show in front of people. They were wearing a mask which covered up their real hearts. With this in mind, we know that the teachings of Jesus aim to reveal our hearts, calling us in repentance and faith before Him. He calls us to come to His Father, who is good and knows our needs (v. 8). By this, Jesus encourages us into reconciliation with the Father. As the chapter continues, Jesus brings up fasting and also talks about those who fast to be seen, which is further exposing this tendency in fallen humans to use worship as a means to an end that is not God, instead, it is man-centered.

THAT'LL PREACH

In verse 7, Jesus warns His followers not to pursue His Father with disingenuous works and words; specifically, He refers to prayers that were overloaded with words and meaningless repetition to "be heard" by others. He describes this as babbling or mumbling. It makes me think of the so-called "mumble rap" genre of our day, in which rappers seemingly utter incoherent words and use synthetic sound distortion, repeating themselves over and over. For older hip-hop fans, we may lament these sounds we don't understand. Regardless of your musical taste, God is not bound to the musical genre, but He does demand our genuineness as we approach Him and understand our words matter, as well as and more importantly, so do our hearts. In the Greek, Jesus uses the word *battalogeo* (ba-ta-low-GEH-oh), which originally pronounced is an onomatopoetic term, which means it is a word that sounds like what it is (e.g., our word "sizzle" makes the sound of something sizzling). Onomatopoetic words are used for rhetorical effect. Jesus is saying they babble. It is meaningless repetition. Such verbosity in prayer was common among the pagans, who thought God could be buttered up. Of course, we worship a God who will not be manipulated (Psalm 115:2–8), and thus when we come to Him it is not to butter Him up for something we want or to use Him to make ourselves look spiritual; rather, it is to humble ourselves before Him and seek His will.

CONCLUSION

If we are honest with ourselves, our spirituality has not always reflected the kind of selfless and God-focused attitude Jesus has described in our study of Matthew 6. It's important to admit this, not as a matter of religious guilt, but rather to bring us to an understanding of the Gospel. The bottom line is, we need Jesus and the ministry of the Holy Spirit if we are to rightly obey this very important teaching, as we come in the worship of the Father. As we meditate on Jesus' teaching, we also need to reflect on His life. He never made almsgiving or prayers to be seen. In the Gospels, Jesus prayed in secret, and He gave to people and told them to keep it on the down low (cf. Mark 1:34, 3:11–12, 8:1–4). Our Lord perfectly obeyed the law of God and gave His life for us. After He ascended, the Lord sent the Spirit, further empowering us for life and mission.

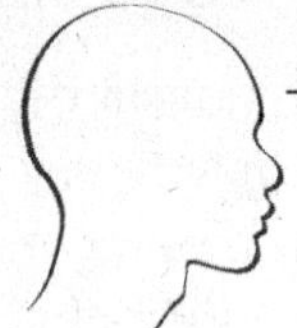

The Disciple's Prayer

By Rev. Dr. Matthew C. Jones

Lesson Theme	Unit Theme	Scripture
The Prayer of Jesus	Jesus Teaches About True Worship	Matthew 6:9–15

INTRODUCTION

Jesus' short prayer in Luke 11 and Matthew 6 (cf. Mark 11:25–26) is perhaps one of the most famous and often recited sections of Jesus' teachings. As a matter of church cultural convention and nomenclature, many refer to it as the "Lord's Prayer." However, this title is not in the original text of these Gospels, and further, it is not actually precise. More accurately, in these verses, we see Jesus teaching His disciples about prayer. In other words, it is not His prayer; rather, it is to be their prayer. He gives them not so much the "Lord's Prayer," but really it is the "Disciple's Prayer." In Matthew 6:9 and Luke 11:1, Jesus tells them, "After this manner therefore pray ye," which shows He is instructing them. What follows is a prayer for them to follow as His disciples. Since Matthew 6 is longer than Luke 11, let's reflect on the wording of this prayer for the disciples and pay careful attention to what follows the liturgy Jesus gives them.

MESSAGE POINTS

Message Point 1: "Prayer to the Father" (Matthew 6:9)

The prayer Jesus gave His disciples, opens with, "Our Father which art in heaven" (Matthew 6:9). He instructed them to pray to God as their Father. It is important to realize this instruction is an amazing invitation to call on our Lord's own Father as ours. It reminds us that in our sin we are alienated from our Creator, and it is only by way of adoption that we can become children of God (Ephesians 1:5, 1 John 3:1–2). Jesus is pointing His disciples to the grace of God with this prayer as it begins. After instructing them to call on God as Father, Jesus tells them to hallow the name of the Lord, which means to keep it holy (cf. Psalm 111:9; Isaiah 5:16; 29:23). In the Hebrew Bible, the promised people were said to hallow God's name by living righteously, and the opposite of this was true as well—that is, if they walked in sin they were profaning His name (cf. also Jeremiah 34:16; Ezekiel 13:19; Amos 2:7). So then, the "Disciple's Prayer" begins with a call to holiness before the holy God, who invites sinners to be sons.

Message Point 2: "Petitions of the Faithful" (vv. 10-13)

As children of the Father, Jesus gives His disciples a liturgy with deep theology that drives intercession. They are instructed to pray for God's kingdom to come to the earth (v. 10a). Going back to the verse before with the language of hallowing God's name, it is important to point out the Hebrew Bible taught God's name would be "hallowed" in the end, when His kingdom would come (Isaiah 29:23; Ezekiel 36:23; 39:7; cf. Zechariah 14:9). As they waited for this prophesied Messianic kingdom, the people were to commit themselves to God's will. In line with this, Jesus says, "Your will be done, On earth as it is in heaven" (v. 10b). Although the world is fallen, we are to seek God's will and also His provision. Jesus further teaches His disciples to seek the Father for the deliverance of temptation/trials and evil (or the evil one). Like the language of hallowing, in the Hebrew Bible, this language has eschatological overtones of the last days when darkness would increase, trials would come and evil would be overthrown. Until that day comes though, the disciples are to be the church on mission, extending grace to the world.

Message Point 3: "Public Forgiveness" (vv. 14-15)
Verses 14 and 15 serve as an appendix to the prayer for the disciples. In these verses, Jesus calls them to give grace to others, as He describes the disciples walking in forgiveness. Here we see Jesus elaborating on the last phrase of Matthew 6:12, "as we forgive our debtors." He later repeated this lesson to His disciples in other places of His teachings (cf. Mark 11:19–26). To be clear, Jesus was not teaching that believers earned God's forgiveness by forgiving others, for this would be contrary to God's free grace and mercy. However, if we have truly experienced God's forgiveness, then we will have a readiness to forgive others (Ephesians 4:32; Colossians 3:13). While some skeptical people view prayer as a religious excuse for inactivity, Jesus' prayer flows into action as disciples are called to forgiveness of humans and active trust in God.

THAT'LL PREACH

In verse 11, the disciples are being called to trust God for their daily bread. Keep in mind, this is not our modern world. Back then, food was not readily available twenty-four hours a day. They didn't have drive-through fast-food places, mega-marts, grocery stores, or even corner markets, not to mention they did not have refrigerators for storing food. They had to make their food for the day, because it could not be stored, and it didn't have the chemicals we pump into our foods to keep them looking fresh longer. Bread was baked each day to meet the needs of that day. People in that culture lived day by day, and much of the day was devoted to finding food. This gives us a sobering reality check to pause and ask ourselves what we are living for and whom we are trusting in our daily life. As we honestly answer this, it gives us a call to come in repentance and faith seeking the tender mercies of our Lord and going to His Father in this prayer He has given us.

CONCLUSION

Jesus longs for us to have this kind of reliance on His Father, which He modeled in His own trial in the wilderness when He fasted forty days and forty nights and yet feasted on the Word of God (Matthew 4:1–11). He enjoyed sweet fellowship with the Father in prayer. So as we think of ways we can be better in prayer or trust God more, we must cling to the Gospel that gives us our standing and power. Thinking of forty days and forty nights in the wilderness, we are reminded of the Israelites who were given manna in the wilderness and yet complained, but once again we juxtapose this with Jesus, who joyfully went without and trusted His Father through it all. He is truly the perfect Savior for His people, bringing us out of the wildness of darkness into the light with the promise of a paradise that is to come. Thy kingdom come.

NOTES

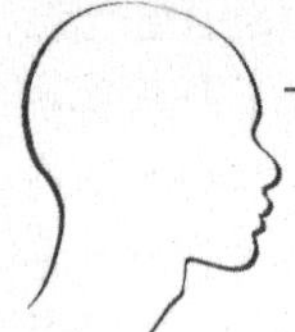

Keep At It!

By Rev. John Burton Jr.

Lesson Theme	Unit Theme	Scripture
Perseverance in Prayer	Jesus Teaches About True Worship	Luke 11:5–13

INTRODUCTION

Prayer is the main method of communication for people of faith. If you have ever been in a room when someone shares their testimony of how God finally answered their prayer after weeks or months of waiting, it's electric! A mixture of celebration, relief, and encouragement fills the atmosphere. Their testimony serves as a source of inspiration for the recipient as well as those aware of the person's highly anticipated request. How do you respond when God hasn't answered your prayer? You did the same, if not more, than others who've had their prayers answered. Your requests were equally as earnest, consistent, and specific, but still, God leaves your request unfulfilled. As a result, you are dumbfounded, dismayed, and dejected about what to do next. Even the most conscientious Christian couldn't help but become a bit discouraged whenever their prayers go unanswered. Thoughts of, "Maybe I should stop praying" begin to percolate in the mind. On the heels of learning the Lord's Prayer, Jesus in this passage instructs on what to do when it seems like our prayers aren't being heard.

MESSAGE POINTS

Message Point 1: "The Predicament" (Luke 11:5–8)

The predicament in Jesus' parable was about a need being met. The nameless man's request wasn't unusual—a need for bread—but his timing was unconventional: midnight. Interestingly, the man wasn't concerned about his personal need but for the need of someone else, his guest. To appear at someone's home at midnight to make a request took boldness even by today's standards. It wasn't his selfishness at the forefront but his urgency to extend hospitality to someone else. After overcoming his neighbor's audacity at such an hour, the man offers a reply. His response was not from his front door but from his bedroom. After hearing no response, the needy neighbor didn't budge. He remained, asking again. This stressed the request's importance. Although the neighbor may not have initially viewed the man's need as vital, he recognized the man's boldness and persistence as attributes to be rewarded. The neighbor realized the man at the door was not willing to take "no" as his final answer. As a result, the neighbor was willing to be inconvenienced, if only for a moment, to carry out the man's request. If this was what the man was willing to do for a friend, what more would God care to do for us?

Message Point 2:"The Process" (vv. 9–10)

According to Newton's third law of motion, "For every action, there is an equal and opposite reaction." This works in faith also. We cannot be passive in our petitions but should be persistent with our pleas. Jesus used action words: ask, seek, and knock to reiterate that Christians should have an active faith. We are to put our faith to work! It's one thing to ask—that's lip service—but to knock and seek—that's action. People make requests all the time.

Most times the requests are meaningful, whereas at other times they aren't. Some requests are filled with personal motives or things that aren't good for us. To test our seriousness and persistence, Jesus suggests putting action behind your words. It's not to seek God to answer every request. But if you seek God, find Him and His will matches our desire, He will grant it in due time. It's the process. Our actions must reinforce the prayers that we offer. The old idiom says, "Actions speak louder than words." We must be willing to commit ourselves through both effort and energy daily to seek God. Are you more interested in the request being fulfilled or the God of the request being pleased?

Message Point 3: "The Perspective" (vv.11–13)

It can become discouraging when you see the ungodly prosper. They have the latest and greatest, never get the diagnosis or disease, and evade their well-merited pink slip. It's as if they are being rewarded for living recklessly. Jesus speaks to this notion with three words, "How much more." If those who are ungodly know how to give good gifts, God's gifts are so much better! His gifts are good and perfect (James 1:17). God does hear and answer our prayers. However, He promises to supply our needs and not necessarily the wants (Philippians 4:19). If you are in tune with the Holy Spirit, you will desire what God desires. His model prayer declares, "not my will but His will be done." God-desired gifts offer long-term spiritual benefits. He is like a loving parent, with a plate of vegetables at dinner time. It may not be what you want, but it's what's good and beneficial. Providing things that aren't profitable or won't matter in the greater picture only puts one in harms' way (vv. 11–12). God won't always cater to your wants, so you will sense that's not all that you need. Later you realize you needed more than what you asked. That's good parenting!

THAT'LL PREACH

Imagine spending thirty years on death row in a five-by-eight-foot cell for a crime you did not commit. This was Anthony Ray Hinton's story. He was convicted of the murder of two fast-food restaurant managers in two separate incidents. Yet, there were no witnesses or fingerprints that linked Hinton to either crime. His formidable defense was a verifiable alibi and a passed polygraph test. Still, he was convicted. Hinton's sole question was, "Why me?" Daily he prayed while thinking that not only did the criminal justice system fail him but wondering if God failed him too. Initially discouraged, Hinton still held on to his truth and steadfastness in God. As he continued to pray, his faith strengthened. Later Hinton joined forces with the Equal Justice Initiative. After studying the case intently, they were able to prove the gun evidence was incorrect. Even after proving so, Hinton still spent an additional ten years in prison. He continued praying. Hinton kept the faith and was eventually released. He persisted in faith! "When every court was saying 'no,' I believe God was still saying yes," Hinton said. When all indications suggested he give up, Hinton kept praying, and his persistence paid off!

CONCLUSION

If you ever had to spend the night at a hotel, draped on the inside doorknob is a sign that reads "Do Not Disturb." It signals to all to not interrupt. Thankfully God never displays this sign for us. In fact, He strongly suggests, keep knocking! Be persistent in bombarding heaven for His attention. If He doesn't answer right away, the first or second day, keep at it!

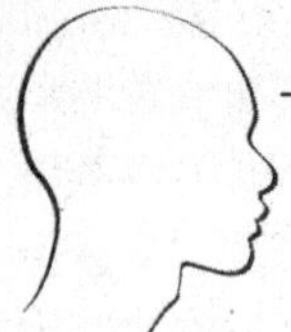

Called to Accountability

By Pastor Gabby Cudjoe-Wilkes

Lesson Theme	Unit Theme	Scripture
Called to Accountability	God Requires Justice	Amos 5:18–24

INTRODUCTION

This passage is a warning for all of us. God is not moved by our festivals or our regular displays of pomp and circumstance. God is invested in justice. God is invested in what we actually do in the name of the Lord, not the things we do that we claim are in God's name but are really our own selfish desires to put on a show, without backing up our ceremonies with our pursuit of justice and righteousness. This passage is difficult because it challenges the things that we have grown accustomed to offering God such as our assemblies, our offerings, and our songs. Some would at first glance think this means that God is not impressed with our church services but that would be too surface of a reading. This is a passage that requires our attentive sensitivity to what is actually being said here. If this is what God hates, then what does God love?

MESSAGE POINTS

Message Point 1: "Check Your Assumptions" (Amos 5:18–20)
This passage begins by talking to those who desire the day of the Lord to hurry toward them. The prophet asks why they want to rush it because the day that looms is a day of gloom, not brightness. This, I believe, is a word to all of us who have become a bit too self-satisfied with our own forms of worship. For those of us who perform our rituals so regularly, we simply assume that we are doing what God desires without checking in with Him. We are making assumptions that God is pleased with our work and our worship, and our assumptions have the capacity to be wrong. The prophet Amos offers a reality check to those who think that God is completely satisfied with everything they are offering. Amos makes the harsh observation that they have a good deal of work to do between now and the day of the Lord, so they really should not rush it. Too often we rest on our laurels and assume we are pleasing God. The harsh truth, however, is that God often is not pleased with our offerings.

Message Point 2: "You or God?" (vv. 21–22)
A gripping pronoun that God uses is "your." "I hate, I despise *your* festivals, and I take no delight in *your* solemn assemblies. Even though you offer me *your* burnt offerings and grain offerings I will not accept them." What a hard thing it is to read this passage and to see that God does not even claim ownership over the festivals and assemblies that the people offer. God does not say my festivals or my assemblies, but He says your. This distant pronoun proves that everything the people were doing was for themselves and not for God. How often do we pat ourselves on the back and focus on carnal metrics of ecclesial impact such as offerings or church attendance? But when we take the focus off of God, God does not even claim the work that we are doing as His own. Instead,

God names it as our work. Our festivals. Our assemblies. How horrific would it be to do all of this work in God's name, and God refuses to even look at it because we have made it all about us.

Message Point 3: "But Let Justice ..." (v. 24)

There is something that God desires and requires, something that God prefers to the rigor of our weekly rituals: God desires justice. God desires righteousness. In one's pursuit of justice and righteousness, one cannot hide one's own motives or selfish ambition. Justice and righteousness require an individual to look beyond the needs of self and see the needs of all. This is the work that the Lord wants us to pursue. And the Lord desires for it to flow like water in a stream. That means that it would be free and accessible to as many as desire it. That kind of world is one that will take a full court press from God's people to bring to fruition. This is the work that pleases God. This is the work that is in the name of the Lord.

THAT'LL PREACH

I'm reminded of the story of a young man who was getting ready to graduate from college. All he wanted as a graduation gift was a new car. On the day he was to graduate his father called him into his private study, told him how proud he was to have such a fine son and how much he loved him. He then handed him a beautifully wrapped gift box. In the box was the son's graduation gift: a Bible with his name on it. "With all of your money, you give me a Bible rather than the sports car I wanted." He then stormed out of the house, leaving the Bible behind. The son didn't talk to his father again. At the time of his father's passing the son went to collect his things. He saw the old graduation gift and finally opened the Bible. Suddenly a key dropped from the back of the Bible. It had a tag on it with the car dealer's name, the same dealer who had the sports car that he wanted so badly for his college graduation. On the tag was the date of his graduation and the words written in large print, "PAID IN FULL."

CONCLUSION

In life, we all have assumptions about what we want and what we think others in our lives want. Israel thought they were honoring God with their festivals and assemblies, but they learned that God was more interested in the work of justice. The young man in our illustration was so one-track minded about the car that he missed out on getting to know his father in the last years of his father's life, and he missed out on the car he wanted so bad. In life, we have to continually check our motives against why we do what we do. We cannot allow ourselves to simply fall into patterns of repetition. Too much is at stake. We suffer greatly when we get it wrong. God is after our desire to do His will. Nothing less will do.

NOTES

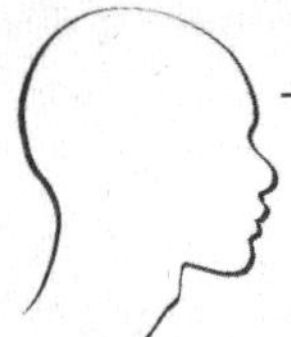

Do I Matter?

By Rev. John Burton Jr.

Lesson Theme	Unit Theme	Scripture
A Prayer for Justice	God Requires Justice	Habakkuk 1:1–4, 12–14

INTRODUCTION

The last six words of the United States' Pledge of Allegiance state, "with liberty and justice for all." In today's world, especially for people of darker hues, we often wonder if this sentiment remains true. Almost daily newscasts, newspapers, and online news postings seem to echo the same message: not all lives matter. It appears Lady Justice's blindfold has vanished, and she's utilizing the very criteria she's supposed to omit to bring about fairness. Impartiality seems to no longer be enforced but instead is exchanged for justice based on wealth, power, or other societal statuses. As a result, the wicked appear to be winning. Although this is the twenty-first century, this mirrors the injustice and wickedness in Habakkuk's time. Wrongdoers went unpunished, and the unjust went without reprimand. Habakkuk's cry for justice to God echoes what many are asking today, "Do I Matter?" Then you wonder, "Where is God?" The one who is never supposed to leave you nor forsake you and the very present help in time of trouble. You pray, but heaven remains silent. Then you are left to wonder, "Do I still matter to God?"

MESSAGE POINTS

Message Point 1: "Don't You Hear Me?" (Habakkuk 1:1–2)

Habakkuk's cry for justice to God sounds much like what many are asking today, "How long?" He was fed up by all the cries to God without a response. So, in a last-ditch effort, he inquired, "How long?" Habakkuk knew that everything has a time limit. There is a time for everything under the sun (Ecclesiastes 3:1). Yet Habakkuk thought this was taking longer than usual. Therefore, he wanted to know when this would be over. Each of us wants God to answer us. But when God remains mute, we think He is not concerned. Like Habakkuk, many hate to feel ignored. When our petitions fall on deaf ears, assumptions usually arise. "Is it me?" "Is my request too big?" "Is God really in control?" Questioning is a logical pattern of thinking when we hear nothing at all. Even in silence, there is always a reason to hope. God's concept of time and man's differ. God could be orchestrating something for your benefit, and in impatience, you ask Him to hurry up. Although Habakkuk was saying, "Save us," God's silence was saying, "Not yet." There will come a time when the cries of sinful will be served justice and the oppressed will be vindicated. But in God's time.

Message Point 2: "Don't You Care?" (vv. 3–4)

Observing his surroundings, Habakkuk progresses in his line of questioning from "How long?" to "Why?" Still, he received the same response, silence. While Habakkuk doesn't pause his questioning and lamenting, to his credit, he still knew to take his concerns to God. Even with what he was witnessing around him and how downtrodden he felt, he has enough wherewithal to know only God has the power to make things right. Habakkuk knew for God to let injustice and wickedness occur, there had to be a reason. When you are dealing with the sovereign God, the maker of the universe, things are a little different than we expect. "For my thoughts are not your thoughts, neither are your ways my ways, saith the LORD" (Isaiah 55:8). What some perceive as God ignoring us may actually be preparation for redemption. In times of deafening silence, are you willing to still talk to God? God could be testing your patience and perseverance. He could be preparing things behind the scenes without your knowledge. In impatience, we want our will to be done rather than God's. Justice may not be in paralysis; it could be in preparation.

Message Point 3: "God Knows" (vv. 12–14)

When life is in flux and it appears the unjust are triumphing, know God is aware. He is omniscient, all-knowing. Despite appearances, something else may actually be occurring. In the eyes of Habakkuk and others, it appears that God has permitted the wickedness and shirked justice for the righteous. Not only has He allowed it, but He has also allowed it to go unpunished, so they think. The heinous too probably believe they have gotten away with wrongdoing. Rather than stop, they continue their assault. In their naiveté, Babylon fails to realize they are simply being used by God to carry out His purpose for Israel. While God allows sin to happen, He never approves of it. Babylon will still be held responsible for their sin and wickedness. God makes evildoers' purposed evil eventually become good (Genesis 50:20). Greed, prosperity, cruelty, and injustice will only last for a while. God never glosses over evil. Vengeance is always God's, and He will administer justice (Romans 12:19). God always has a way of reversing the roles in favor of the righteous. Righteousness always prevails!

THAT'LL PREACH

Michael Brown, Trayvon Martin, Keith Lamont Scott, and Sandra Bland are a few of the names of victims who were killed by police or died while in police custody unjustifiably. In many of the instances, law enforcement offered unconvincing explanations for their actions. In cases where video evidence was presented, viewers deduced the officers' actions were not justified but still led to an acquittal. Their families, the general public, and a host of others are left wondering, "Where is God and why would He allow this to happen?" This common question is ranked high like the time-honored, "Why do bad things happen to good people?" These unfortunate incidents are becoming more commonplace, resulting in raw emotions, the heightened sensitivity with law enforcement, and distrust of the justice system. Still, remain hopeful. Not because the systems of this world will work themselves out but because God will execute His justice. There will always be wicked people in power perverting justice for their benefit. God is from everlasting to everlasting and will leave no bad deed unpunished.

CONCLUSION

Do you matter? Yes! Habakkuk complained and possibly doubted, but he never gave up hope. What he witnessed, heard, and felt were troubling, if not traumatizing. Still, he prayed to God for justice. Habakkuk knew God would never abandon His people. Society will never be fair. The scales of justice will constantly become unbalanced. Still, go to God for help. Even if it appears He doesn't hear your cries, understand injustice never goes unpenalized. On the day of judgment, God is the final judge who issues proper punishment.

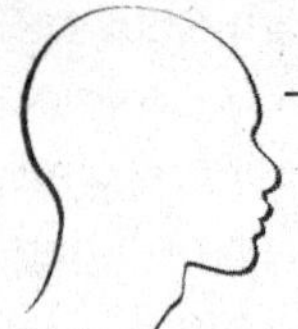

Two Birds, One Stone

By Geno Olison

Lesson Theme	Unit Theme	Scripture
Consequences for Injustice	God Requires Justice	Habakkuk 2:6–14

INTRODUCTION

It's true that life can seem so unfair at times. It can often be a real struggle to trust and delight in our Heavenly Father when evil men and women seem to suffer none of the unpleasant consequences of their actions. The psalmist, Asaph, says it best in Psalm 73: "For I was envious at the foolish, when I saw the prosperity of the wicked. For there are no bands in their death: but their strength is firm … They are corrupt, and speak wickedly concerning oppression: they speak loftily." Like us, Asaph struggled to understand how God could be so negligent and not simply crush the evildoers. As we get to know God more, especially through the Scriptures, we ultimately find that He is a God of justice and—despite how it might seem at times—no one is slick enough to escape His mighty hand. The prophet Habakkuk gets a crash course in both God's sovereignty and justice. Even though the evil Babylonians will be an instrument of God's judgment for Judah, the Babylonians won't be able to escape God's judgment for their own wickedness. This text can teach us a few valuable lessons about wickedness and God's judgment.

MESSAGE POINTS

Message Point 1: "God Can Turn the Tables" (Habakkuk 2:6–7)

God's plan was to use the Babylonians to judge Judah (1:5–6) because they were wicked and cruel enough to be effective. They loved violence and used brutality and corruption to crush anyone they set their sights on. Despite God's willingness to use them for His purposes, He despises their wickedness and vows to soon bring an end to it. The Babylonians were used to having their way with their victims, but God promises that eventually the tables would turn and the captives would taunt and mock their captors. We also learn that there is an economic aspect to this. The Babylonians were known to burden the people with heavy taxation and oppress the poor with loans and excessive interest. When God rains His judgment, the debtors will rise up and plunder their creditors. One of the distinguishing marks of God's promise of justice is that He not only stops the oppression, but He lifts up the underdog and shifts the power and wealth with sudden reversals of fortune. God can, and often does, turn the tables.

Message Point 2: "Nothing Can Stop the Mighty Hand of God" (vv. 9–12)

Power, often fueled by wealth, can seem to offer us protection from the consequences of our sin. Evil people also tend to have many enemies, which forces them to be vigilant about securing their homes and fortifying their cities. The Babylonians were immensely wealthy because of their cruelty and treachery. With this wealth, they were able to enjoy security. It's true that many of us get rather good at being bad, and if we've been at it for a while, we might feel untouchable. We might be able to talk, intimidate, or flirt our way out of trouble with other people, but it's a whole other ball game when it comes to God Almighty. No amount of money, influence, powerful friends, or military might is able to protect us from Yahweh. This is a helpful reminder for all of us that we can never get good enough at sin that God can't humble us. He promises to bring them down and nothing will stop Him.

Message Point 3: "God Makes Them Aware of His Glory" (vv. 13–14)

It's helpful and necessary to know that God is purposeful in all that He does. He also has a unique way of killing multiple birds with a single stone. This whole storyline is evidence of God's divine ability to accomplish whatever he wants. Judah is judged, the Babylonians are humbled, and through it all, all those involved experience a heightened awareness of God's glory, power, and might. When God's people are reminded of who He is (even through His punishment), God wins. When those who defy the armies of God are humbled by His mighty hand, God wins. When the casual observers of these events behold God doing His thing, God wins. Why? Because His glory is on display, and an awareness of that glory is raised in the eyes and hearts of everyone involved. God and God alone can humble His beloved people and their seemingly untouchable enemies. When the wicked are humbled, God's glory shines.

THAT'LL PREACH

We live in a world where injustice is always on display. Powerful people abuse the vulnerable and often seem to get away with it. Rich politicians and celebrities often seem to live by different rules. In the world's economy, especially with its obsession with celebrity and fame, wealth and influence seem to insulate the powerful from the natural consequences of their bad behavior. However, in God's economy, Paul's words in Galatians 6:7 should anchor our understanding of how God deals with the unrepentant: "Be not deceived; God is not mocked: for whatsoever a man soweth, that shall he also reap." It may not happen soon or even on this side of eternity, but God is just, and He can handle His business.

CONCLUSION

It's true that God is up to a lot in this world. His wisdom, justice, power, mercy, and love are working at the same time, which makes Him uniquely qualified to run the world. We are tasked with trusting that God knows exactly what He's doing and that no matter how it might appear, both the righteous and the wicked will get what they have coming. No one can or will escape the hand of God. Even in His wrath and displeasure, His glory is put on display. Be comforted and humbled by the knowledge that God's justice simply can't be mocked.

NOTES

____

____

____

____

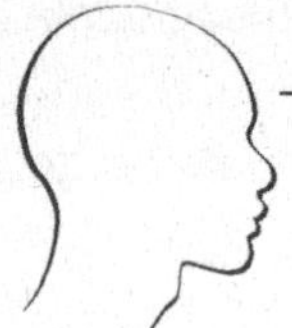

The More Important Things

By Howard Lee Thomas III, MDiv

Lesson Theme	Unit Theme	Scripture
Corrupt Leaders	God Requires Justice	Micah 3:1–3, 9–12; 6:6–8

INTRODUCTION

At first, Israel was one kingdom, and David was its king. God made a covenant with David to always prosper Israel and have a descendant of David as their king. Jesus is the ultimate heir of this covenant as are all peoples through Jesus by faith. However, David's adultery with Bathsheba and coverup murder of her husband Uriah grieved God, and God proceeded to split Israel into two kingdoms (Judah and Israel) by a series of unfortunate events. Judah would always have a descendant of David as king and thus remain in God's covenant but would stray into injustice and idolatry. Micah was one of a number of prophets to speak against the injustice of Judah from approximately 737 to 696 BC. Themes of liberation and justice from unjust leaders are strong in Micah's writings. Micah's example of confronting powerful leaders who have oppressed and neglected the less-powerful and weak is a timeless one for those seeking societal reform. This sermon addresses how to confront fallen leaders with God's Word.

MESSAGE POINTS

Message Point 1: "The Powerful That Prey Instead of Pray" (Micah 3:1–3)

A systemic issue of a nation that is not turned toward the Lord is self-seeking and lost leaders who enact unjust, unwise, and even harsh policies upon their fellow citizens. Knowing right from wrong and having a higher calling to love selflessly and sacrificially makes for good leadership. Not having these values makes for leaders who use people for their own selfish ambitions. To this Micah says, "And I said, Hear, I pray you, O heads of Jacob, and ye princes of the house of Israel; Is it not for you to know judgment? Who hate the good, and love the evil; who pluck off their skin from off them, and their flesh from off their bones" (Micah 3:1–2). The words here are strong and direct. Micah would have visually witnessed the violence of godless injustice toward the poor and oppressed in Judah, and he spoke out in protest. Sin is essentially cannibalism, which is Cain-Abel-ism, where we destroy and devour our own. The church and each of its members must expose that sin does this and ask, "How is sin devouring our community, nation, family, and so on?"

Message Point 2: "Seduction Leads to Corruption" (vv. 9–12)

Micah goes deeper into what the atmosphere is like for a leader who is being led into the sin of corrupt and oppressive leadership. Oftentimes it is money and a delusional sense of a moral superiority that leads to leaders becoming oppressors, users, and devourers. To this point Micah says, "The heads thereof judge for reward, and the priests thereof teach for hire, and the prophets thereof divine for money: yet will they lean upon the LORD, and say, Is not the LORD among us? none evil can come upon us" (3:11). When people in power resort to oppressive and exploitative acts, they often believe they are in a position that gives them a moral or ethical right to do so. Micah challenges this by putting leaders, like all people, under the scope of God's will, which is love and justice. Asking "what lies are being told and what is the truth?" is vital in exposing predators in the darkness.

Message Point 3: "Good Leaders Are Good Followers" (Micah 6:6–8)

Micah gives a solution to oppressive leaders who, due to sin, are destroying their community by "Cain-Abel-ism." He calls leaders to be like the ones they have been called to lead: followers of God. He says, "He hath shewed thee, O man, what is good; and what doth the LORD require of thee, but to do justly, and to love mercy, and to walk humbly with thy God" (Micah 6:8). Micah says the solution to ending predatory leadership is to require leaders' primary focus to be on justice, love, and mercy over providing physical needs. Micah positions the center of how to be a good leader on love, empathy, and the moral conscience all being submitted to God in humility. Whom are you submitted to as you are also leading others and is that person you follow submitted to God in love?

THAT'LL PREACH

A few years ago, I watched a movie starring actor Bradley Cooper called *American Sniper*, which is based on a true story of American soldier Chris Kyle. In the film Cooper, plays a sniper soldier in the Middle East with specific missions and targets to eliminate. The movie addresses the moral issue of whether a sniper can be a true hero or is simply a coward since they are not directly in the battlefield. Chris Kyle addresses this moral dilemma by the statement, "The sheep need protection from wolves. Wolves prey on the sheep. Sheepdogs protect the sheep from wolves. I am a sheepdog." Cooper's character is often in positions where he is watching from a distance, ready to shoot when a danger (or a wolf) enters among sheep. He has to identify whether the danger is real or not—if it is a sheep or not—and take action. Chris Kyle is often still in danger and has to evade enemy snipers to do his job.

CONCLUSION

As Christians, we are to expose wolves with the Gospel and the life of Jesus Christ. If sin and lies are allowed to persist in the land, then essentially the people we love will become victims of its effects, which also include oppressive leadership. Micah was essentially a sheepdog and was willing to speak out against injustice by having the right "scope," the Word and will of God centered in justice, love, and mercy. Let the church similarly be compelled, in love and Gospel truth, to dive into the Word of God, pray, and confront leaders who do not love God.

NOTES

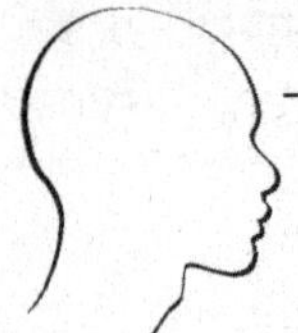

Leading by God's Example

By Allen Reynolds, MDiv

Lesson Theme	Unit Theme	Scripture
Leading Justly	God Requires Justice	Malachi 2:1–9; 3:5–6

INTRODUCTION

There is great temptation to believe you are always right when you are in charge. There is even greater temptation to believe you are always right when you want to be in charge. Being a leader is difficult; the risks you take and the moves you make affect not only you but everyone you lead. As followers of Christ, our lives are even harder because we are all called to be leaders. We are called to lead justly, whether at home, work, in our congregations, in our communities, or in our nations. Malachi reminds us that today, leaders are under great judgment from the Lord for how they lead. Those who lead with God leading them will bring more abundance to life. But those who lead without submitting to God's wisdom are headed toward destruction with people following right behind.

MESSAGE POINTS

Message Point 1: "Be Led by the Lord" (Malachi 2:1–4)

As leaders and as believers we must be led by the Lord. The Israelite priests Malachi is prophesying against had gotten far away from God's will by refusing to follow God's lead. The priests were not keeping the requirements of being good priests, offering cheap sacrifices as well as spreading false teaching and stealing from the people. They were supposed to lead the people as righteous examples, yet they couldn't even live right themselves. They refused to honor God and treated their service to the Lord as a cheap afterthought. People desired God's truth, and the priests were teaching them convenient lies. The Lord was disgusted with them. A disgusting image is used to express the force of His disgust: their faces should be covered with feces, and they should be thrown in the trash. When God calls us to repent and lead justly, He is serious about it. He will make even our blessings turn into curses and allow us to be humiliated until we recognize that all blessings come from Him and He is worthy of all honor, not us.

Message Point 2: "Be Taught by the Past" (vv. 5–7)

Malachi reminds the priests of the good examples of the past and the purpose of the priesthood itself. The priest is supposed to be a messenger of God. When the priests obey God, they bring life and peace to the people they lead. We know just leaders by the fruit that follows them. The good priests of the past did what was just, walked with God, and led others to walk in justice. The priests did their best to honor God and teach the people truth. As Proverbs 29:2 says "When the righteous are in authority, the people rejoice: but when the wicked beareth rule, the people mourn." Justice is tangible.

Message Point 3: "Be Moved to Repentance" (Malachi 2:8–9, 3:5–6)

God wants the priests to know the impact of their twisted leadership and the judgment awaiting them. He is holding them accountable for the people doing wrong because they were taught wrong. The priests thought they were getting away with using their position to serve themselves and ignoring God's law. But the people they were leading weren't stupid. God would reveal what was happening and cause them to be humiliated for their discrimination in whom they served. But all leaders would be judged, not just the priests. God would bear witness on behalf of the oppressed. The poor, the foreigner, the worker, the widow, and the orphan who had been taken advantage of by unjust leaders would all receive God's justice. The bad leaders would face judgment. God has always been a God of justice; He has not changed and will not allow unjust leadership to go on.

THAT'LL PREACH

There was a little boy who loved to play in the water of the creek by his house. But one day when he went to play he noticed that the water was bloody. He looked around and didn't see anything bleeding in the creek so he wondered where the blood was coming from. He went to tell his father and have him check it out. His father looked at the scene and told him to follow him. As they walked up the creek, they found a wounded deer bleeding nearby. The boy asked his father how he knew where the blood was coming from. His father replied, "When there is a problem downstream, it normally starts upstream."

CONCLUSION

When we see widespread sickness in our nations, our communities, our churches, and our homes, we need to check on our leadership, not to point fingers but to get to the source of the problem. God calls us to just leadership that cares for the least of these, not to use our positions to take advantage of them. We are all creations of God. We are all called to serve God together. When we are faithful to lead justly, we allow our followers room to flourish.

NOTES

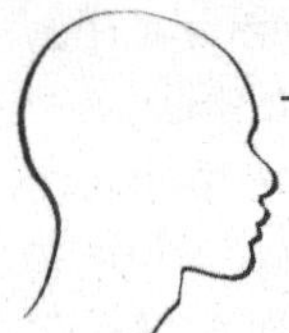

APRIL 5, 2020

A Servant for All

By Allen Reynolds, MDiv

Lesson Theme	Unit Theme	Scripture
God's Just Servant	God Promises a Just Kingdom	Isaiah 42:1–9

INTRODUCTION

Have you ever seen someone you read about or saw on TV in person? Like randomly running into an actor you were a fan of out to dinner? Or spotting an author who really impacted you at a coffee shop? Or a civil rights icon you read about at a church event? You see them and think to yourself, "Wow I know them!" Well, that feeling times a million is what the disciples felt when they realized Jesus was the Messiah. They had grown up reading in their Bibles about the Messiah coming. They had read passages like Isaiah 42 and never thought they would see the day. It had been hundreds of years since those things were written, yet when they recognized Jesus, they knew the writings were talking about Him.

MESSAGE POINTS

Message Point 1: "The Gentle Judge" (Isaiah 42:1–4)

This Servant of God's justice is unlike any other before them. He is called to bring justice to all the nations, and is unrelenting in His distribution of justice. Yet He is also so gentle that he does not crush the weakest reed. How is this possible? We often think of justice as harsh punishment or extended prison sentences. But this judge of the nations executes justice that is gentle and gracious. This justice causes everything to be made right. The poor are cared for. The sick are healed. The abused are restored. The wicked are humbled. Brokenness is made whole. It is hard for us to imagine this judge until we see Jesus. Jesus is unrelenting in calling for right treatment of all people and demonstrating restoration to wholeness from the greatest to the least, while at the same time willing to go to the cross without a word of defense for Himself against false accusations. The disciples see it and recognize He is the servant from Isaiah!

Message Point 2: "The Righteous Liberator" (vv. 5–7)

God is the sovereign Lord of the universe. Everything everywhere is at His command. He has commanded His servant to be a light to the nations. He would send the servant as a symbol of His faithfulness to Israel. God will always keep God's promises. God had promised to redeem His people with His servant. The servant would open the eyes of the blind and set the captives free. Jesus fulfills the prophecy! He opened the eyes of the blind. He liberated the captives. He said He was the light of the world. He was protected by God. Shortly after he began His public ministry, the religious and political leaders wanted to kill Him. But they could not touch Him because God protected Him until He gave Himself to be arrested and killed on the Cross. And He is the redemption for not only Israel but for all people.

Message Point 3: "The Hope of the Future" (vv. 8–9)

God is God. There is no one like God anywhere at any time. God is seated in eternity. God sees the past, present, and future at the same time, all the time. And God has the power to do exactly what He says He will do. He has in fact already done it. Glory to God who sees the end from the beginning and who alone is worthy of our praise! God promised to deliver the Israelites with a righteous judge and He kept His promise delivering us from our bondage to sin and calling us to be His body in continuing to extend His justice to the nations.

THAT'LL PREACH

In 1845, when people read *The Narrative of the Life of Frederick Douglass: An American Slave,* they could not believe a former slave wrote it. For many people, it was the first time they had been exposed to a slave who could write, let alone write with such eloquence. Some people refused to believe he wrote it. Then they heard him speak in person. And they were moved by his speeches and gave to his cause of abolition. Reading about Frederick Douglass was one thing. But when they saw in person what they had read about, it helped to change the nation and support freedom for all the slaves.

CONCLUSION

God was telling people about His servant hundreds of years before His servant appeared in history. Before anyone saw Him in person, they would know how to recognize Him. They read about Him. They heard about Him. And then two thousand years ago, they saw Him. Glory to God! God is faithful! He kept His promise after hundreds of years and in Jesus revealed His righteous judgment of the nations. May people be so moved by our presence, representing the Jesus they have heard about as His living letters, that they support Jesus' call of justice for all people!

NOTES

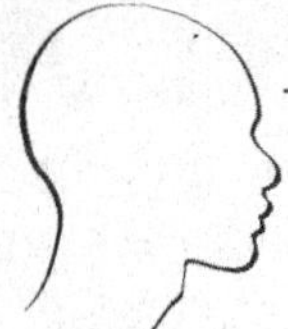

The Power of the Resurrection

By Dr. Stanley Long

Lesson Theme	Unit Theme	Scripture
Resurrection Hope	God Promises a Just Kingdom	1 Corinthians 15:1–8, 12–14, 20–23, 42-45

INTRODUCTION

Easter is either the most successful deception in the history of humanity, or it is the greatest divine expression humanity will ever see. If it is not true, the whole Christian faith is a joke, but if it is true, then one would be wise to contemplate its implications.

MESSAGE POINTS

Message Point 1: "The Resurrection Enhances Our Present Reality" (1 Corinthians 13:1–8)
Paul emphasizes that the preaching of the Gospel enabled the Corinthians to be saved. They had experienced resurrection by believing Paul's message regarding the death, burial, and resurrection of Jesus. To live in this present world without Jesus is to be spiritually dead while one is physically alive. Only a resurrection can enhance our current reality to what God had in mind for His creatures. "I have come that they [you] might have life," said Jesus (John 10:10). Eternal life begins when Jesus resurrects our dead spiritual self to life.

Message Point 2: "The Resurrection Stimulates Our Need for Ongoing Vitality" (v. 22)
Paul says in Christ all will be made alive (v. 22). Although I believe this verse is mostly about our future, Christ makes us alive every present day too. The vitality of the Spirit is crucial to our being able to live out the Christian life day by day. Christ makes that which is dead live, not just once when we are born again, but every day as we encounter all kinds of situations that need life. The criminal justice system needs a resurrection; the local schools that are killing our kids needs a resurrection; our decaying neighborhoods need a resurrection. We can't help dry bones live without the vitality of that resurrected Christ flowing through our resurrected spirits.

Message Point 3: "The Resurrection Ushers in Our Future Finality" (vv. 42–45)
No one will be able to escape the inevitability of death, but Paul's point is that the Resurrection means it is not over for the follower of Christ just because we die. Death meets its Waterloo in Christ's resurrection. Just as Adam's disobedience led the whole human race to death, Christ's obedience leads all of Adam's children to resurrection. The division between God and His children ends. The ongoing struggle between our diseased, decaying, feeble bodies and our inner selves will end. The war will be over, and the battle that death has always won in the past will be someone else's victory.

THAT'LL PREACH

There's an old parable about blind men and an elephant. One man grabs the elephant's tail and says, "It's a brush." Another grabs the elephant's trunk and says, "It's a snake." Another grabs the elephant's ear and says, "It's a fan." Still another grabs the elephant's leg and says, "It's a tree." The lesson is supposed to be that no one knows everything and only if we all listen to each other and fit our ideas together will we come to the truth. In scriptural matters, however, this parable falls flat. We do not believe Christianity because it's the religion we happened to grab that makes sense to us. We believe Christianity because it is true because the Resurrection really happened. We don't need to listen to other religions say, "I believe in only a spiritual resurrection. I believe in reincarnation. I believe we don't have spirits at all," and then harmonize all these views together to understand the truth. We follow Jesus who heals the blind so that anyone can see the whole truth. The truth is Jesus of Nazareth is the Son of God, who really died and was really buried, who really rose from the dead and really appeared to His followers, and who really gives new life to anyone who will accept the reality of His truth.

CONCLUSION

While we know Jesus did all the work of defeating death, we must not pretend we can just sit around and ignore opportunities to battle the lingering effects of death. Paul tells us, "Be ye stedfast, unmoveable, always abounding in the work of the Lord, forasmuch as ye know that your labour is not in vain in the Lord" (from v. 58). The miracle of the Resurrection enhances our present reality and stimulates our need for ongoing vitality. So let us continue the work God has appointed. As the song says:

So until then my heart will go on singing,
So until then with joy I'll carry on,
Until the day my eyes behold the city,
Until the day God calls me home.

NOTES

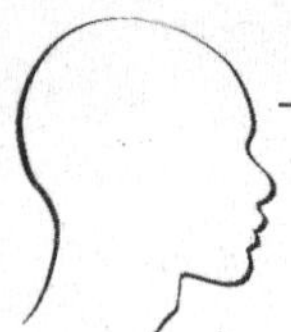

Boomerang Season

By Jerome Gay Jr.

Lesson Theme	Unit Theme	Scripture
Injustice Will Be Punished	God Promises a Just Kingdom	Esther 7:1-10

INTRODUCTION

In 1992, Reginald Hudlin directed *Boomerang*, a movie that captured the essence of reaping and sowing in relationships. The movie starred Eddie Murphy playing a character named Marcus Graham, a very successful advertising executive, and an avid womanizer. In fact, he had an insatiable desire for using women. Marcus would meet his match in Jacqueline Broyer, his new boss played by Robin Givens, essentially a female version of himself. She uses Marcus for her own sexual exploits, and Marcus is confronted with how he made countless women feel, which is why the title of the movie—*Boomerang*—is both appropriate and profound. In our text, Haman has thrown out death, destruction, and denial, and now he'll face judgment and consequences for his actions. He's entering his boomerang season.

MESSAGE POINTS

Message Point 1: "Esther Displays Courage and Compassion" (Esther 7:1–4)

This is the second feast (the first one took place in chapter 5) where Esther could've said something, but she didn't. This made way for Haman having to parade Mordecai around the city. This is the feast of feasts, because it will be Haman's last, and all of his threats, deceit, hate and gossip will come back on him. But before we get there, God wants us to learn from Esther. There are a few attributes we can learn from Esther:

Courage to Confront—This is the second time that Esther put her life on the line, because she understands that she has an assignment for her life given by God, and she's willing to die for it. The first time she put her life on the line was when she approached the king without his summoning her (Esther 4:11, 5:1), and now she's sitting with a king who could kill her on a whim, and Haman, who she knows wants her and all of her people dead. Keep in mind, she's doing this for others. Neither Haman nor the king knows that she's Jewish.

Compassion for the Voiceless—Esther's compassion for the voiceless is in high definition. Here's a young, beautiful, and intelligent young woman who could literally get by on her looks (in fact, she's so beautiful, the king offered her half of the kingdom), but she rejects being a trophy wife, and says, I'm more than my looks, I'm a daughter of The eternal King, Yahweh. Not only that, she chooses to be a voice for others who will suffer at the hands of the current empire. The church should be the first to talk about prison reform, gender equality, the sanctity of life, and other issues because we believe all people are made in His image.

Message Point 2: "Learn the Difference between 'Weed Killer' and 'Fertilizer' Relationships" (v. 5)

King Ahasuerus is baffled because he still doesn't know that Haman played him; he is getting a taste of his own medicine. His lack of compassion and his saying yes to every request he got is coming back to bite him. Remember this: When you let divisive people become your counselors and confidants: "Good people" can be bad company. Remember, your boomerang season will either develop or destroy you depending on what you put out there. Weed killer relationships take, while fertilizer relationships build. King Ahasuerus didn't do this, and now he's shocked. But he shouldn't be. He hasn't sown compassion; he didn't show Vashti compassion when he kicked her out simply for saying, no; he didn't show the other young ladies compassion when he took their virginity and sent them away; and he didn't show the Jewish people compassion when he didn't even take time to read the letter he authorized, which was meant for their destruction. Kill weeds, fertilize grass. This means we confront discord, and we fertilize the unity of the body.

Message Point 3: "God's Justice Will Ultimately Prevail" (vv. 6–10)

One response to injustice doesn't fit all. Mordecai owed forgiveness and reaped the blessing of that decision five years later (between Esther 1 and chapter 2, five years had passed). God will work some situations in our lives like that. Esther has a face-to-face with the one who wanted her and her people dead. Sometimes we're trying to wait some things out that God wants us to confront. In other words, God wants you to sow courage by confronting the person, not because it guarantees a particular response from them, but because it builds character in you. Haman thought he was in control until reality hit, and his fall was quick. It had been several years since he had been in power and it was all taken away in moments. You and I need to think about this regarding how we treat people. Consequences can be swift and severe.

THAT'LL PREACH

Eddie Murphy's character ended up getting what he put out, and we see that Haman experienced a boomerang season that ended in his death. Others have experienced this too: Jacob tricked his brother Esau and his father (Genesis 27:1–30), and he ended up getting tricked by Laban (Genesis 29:14–30). Pharaoh drowned the baby boys (Exodus 1:22), and Pharaoh and his men drowned (Exodus 14:28). Jezebel promised a violent death for Elijah (1 Kings 19:1–3), and she herself had a violent death (2 Kings 9:30–37). Those are boomerang seasons of destruction, but there were also boomerang seasons of blessing: Mordecai saved King Ahasuerus life without him knowing it (Esther 2:19–23), and God saved Mordecai's life without him knowing it (Esther 6:4–5). Esther risked her life for her people (Esther 4:11), and God used her courage to save her people (Esther 8:2).

CONCLUSION

Three things we should consider:

1. We should *confess* instead of trying to avoid consequences. The Bible even tells us there's healing in confession (James 5:16).
2. We should *confront* ourselves, and we'll be able to confront others like Esther had to confronted Haman.
3. We should remember that the God of all justice will win! (Ecclesiastes 12:14)

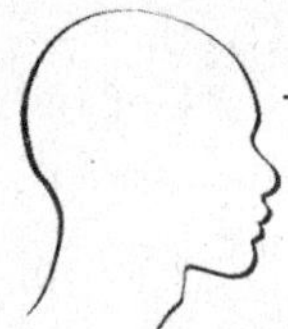

What God Loves the Most

By Ramon Mayo

Lesson Theme	Unit Theme	Scripture
The Lord Loves Justice	God Promises a Just Kingdom	Isaiah 61:8–11; 62:2–4

INTRODUCTION

By the looks of our churches, it would be easy to point out what God loves the most. You can look at the typical American church and think God must be over the top in love with large ornate buildings. You could probably assume the Lord loves worship songs above all else. You could even conclude those whom God loves the most are well-dressed people who have it all together. But such conclusions would be wrong. Above all of the religious things we can do, the Lord loves when we pursue justice. Today I want to talk about what God loves the most.

MESSAGE POINTS

Message Point 1: "What God Loves Most Is Justice for His People" (Isaiah 61:8–9)

In these verses we see God laying down the law. He loves justice, and He hates the opposite of justice: robbery and wickedness. He doesn't want to see His people exploited and oppressed. He wants to see them thrive and prosper. When this happens, everyone in the world will be able to clearly see that God is a great God!

Message Point 2: "What God Loves Most Is Justice for the World" (vv. 10–11)

God makes His people prosper so that the nations can see us. Isaiah describes the shining finery God lavishes on His obedient children, because not only does God love justice for His people, but He also wants justice for the world. There are so many around the globe who are oppressed and taken advantage of. There are so many who are being trafficked as slaves and kidnapped by terrorist groups. It seems like the world is swallowed up by injustice, but the text says God is going to show His justice to the nations of the world! It's our call as His people to follow His example.

Message Point 3: "What God Loves Most Is His Realized Kingdom of Justice" (Isaiah 62:2–4)

Most of the time the cry for justice is attempting to rectify a present injustice. Isaiah points to a time when justice will cover the whole earth. It's a time when the heavenly city will come down like a bride as John speaks about in Revelation. There will be no more oppression, no more injustice. The beauty of God's redemption will cover the world with mercy, justice, and peace. What a day that will be!

THAT'LL PREACH

When children say they love their parents but continue to fight or take advantage of their siblings, their love means nothing. Their parents want them to show love by pursuing their parents' interests and concerns. When we say we love God and choose to sit out the fight against injustice, then we are the same as children who voice their love to their parents verbally but have no idea what their parents are truly concerned about. Paul encourages the Ephesians to instead "be ye therefore followers of God, as dear children" (Ephesians 5:1).

CONCLUSION

God loves justice. This is what He loves most. Our songs and conferences mean nothing if we are not letting justice roll down like water and righteousness like a mighty stream. We can have Christian bumper stickers on our cars and the biggest Bibles we can find. We can dress nicely and shout our praises during church services, but it means nothing without justice. God wants us to pursue justice. This is His top priority.

NOTES

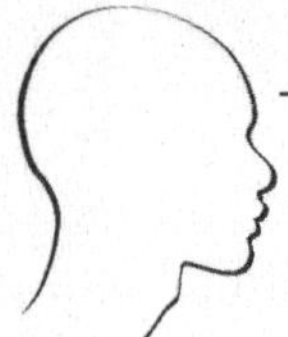

God's Lullaby

By Rev. Porsha D. Williams

Lesson Theme	Unit Theme	Scripture
A Vision of Restoration	Called to God's Work of Justice	Zephaniah 3:14–20

INTRODUCTION

At some point, everyone will feel the weight of the world. Tragedy and turmoil seem to flood the televisions and newspapers. There are times when people begin to wonder if God has plans to intervene. Is God going to do what He has promised? Even after things are lost, God has made the choice to continue to pursue justice. The work of justice is an ongoing endeavor. Justice does not happen overnight, and justice does not look the same in every situation. Yet, justice pushes for God to show up in ways that are needed for His children. God hears the cries of His children, and it is with the intention that God desires to see His children flourish, even in the midst of injustice.

MESSAGE POINTS

Message Point 1: "The Lord Is Present" (Zephaniah 3:14–17)

One of God's promises that we continue to see throughout the biblical text is that God promises to be with us. God is a God who is with His children. That is no different in the book of Zephaniah. In verses 14–17, we see Zephaniah sharing a command for Zion to sing, to be glad, and to rejoice with a full heart because God has taken away Israel's punishment. In addition, God has made their enemy turn away. In the midst of this, Zephaniah reminds Israel that God is present. Therefore, there is no need to fear harm. God is the true King and a mighty warrior, and God's presence is emphasized with royal and majestic imagery. There is no need to believe that God will harm them or that their enemy will harm them at this point because God is over all. God is the one who saves and rescues His people in the time of trouble and turmoil. As a result of God's presence, He joins in with the Israelites with singing as opposed to rebuking them.

Message Point 2: "The Lord Will Deliver" (vv. 18–20)

In the beginning chapters of Zephaniah, God makes a motion to destroy the earth and all who live in it, in reverse of creation. However, by chapter 3, God shows mercy with the intention to deliver the people of Israel as a solution. Instead of destruction, God makes the choice to deliver. This speaks to the sovereignty of God. God could have decided to go through with the original oracle that pushes for removal and disaster. However, He decides not only to deliver but also decides to deal with Israel's enemy. All who are lame will be rescued. God will also "gather the exiles" (v. 19), which is another form of rescue. After being displaced, to be delivered home is something that many want.

Message Point 3: "The Lord Will Restore" (v. 20)

We love a God who is both present and who will deliver His people from the hands of their enemies. In addition, God is also a God who will restore. God does not leave the people without stability or care. In the restoration process, God shows up as a provider. Those who are exiled will be restored and provided for. In addition, in every land that they were put to shame by their enemies, God will see to it that they will receive the praise and the honor that they deserve. God will not only restore the people with goods, but He will also restore reputation and internal well-being. Restoration goes beyond what money can buy. Restoration is a process of becoming whole again. The pieces that were lost and broken are placed back together and resealed by God. The best part is that all will witness this restoration process. God does not desire to hide it from anyone because it ultimately brings God glory.

THAT'LL PREACH

Whatever happened to the lullaby? Back in the day when a child would cry, mothers and fathers would sing lullabies to their children to help them fall asleep. Yet somewhere along the way, the culture has drifted away from the sweet tender sounds of the lullaby. Whatever happened to parents singing sounds of joy for peace? While there may be less singing in homes, God is still singing. The text reminds us that God is a God who not only loves to hear His children sing praises, but God is also a God who loves to sing over His children. God is still singing over us even today with the sounds of joy that cause us to march on. Songs of resistance to evil are being sung over us as we continue to face the injustices of this world. God is a God who continues to sing lullabies of love to remind us that He is always there, ready to restore.

CONCLUSION

In conclusion, God is a God who makes good on His promises. God, who delivers and restores, is ever-present. While God originally had a plan to press the reset button on all of creation, He decided that there was another way to restore Israel. The enemy of the Israelites was prepared to overtake them, yet God saw fit to remove Israel's enemy from them. Through justice, love, and mercy, the Israelites have inherited a new song to sing. God rejoices over His children with singing as they overcome. His children are encouraged to do the same.

NOTES

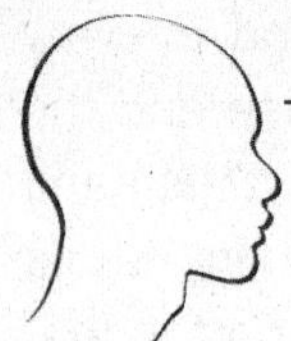

No Justice, No Peace

By Ramon Mayo

Lesson Theme	Unit Theme	Scripture
Peace and Justice Reign	Called to God's Work of Justice	Zechariah 8:1–8, 11–17

INTRODUCTION

I remember it like it was yesterday. The Rodney King trial was underway. It was all over the news, and when you saw the protesters in front of the courthouse, the chant was always the same "No Justice, No Peace!" The protesters then were speaking to a modern-day incident, but when you think about the words of their protest, it makes sense from a biblical point of view. Without justice there can be no peace in this world. God wants to bring justice and transform our world of wars, violence, and oppression into a peaceful kingdom. The title of my message today is "No Justice, No Peace."

MESSAGE POINTS

Message Point 1: "Peace Comes with the Presence of God" (Zechariah 8:1–8)

In this passage Zechariah points to a time when God's people will dwell in safety. He underscores this by stating God's passionate love for His people and how He is one day going to live in His holy city Jerusalem. This will bring about lasting peace. If you want peace in your life, then it has to come from the presence of God. If this world is going to have peace, it's got to come from the presence of God and His rule over the earth.

Message Point 2: "Peace Comes with Economic Prosperity" (vv. 11–13)

God's peace comes with economic prosperity. If you look around at the world today and look back through history, a major source of injustice and war was economic inequality. It is a lack of prosperity causing people to rob and do violence to each other. It is a lack of economic stability causing nations to go to war against other nations. If you look at your own life, when there's more month than money, then you don't have peace. God says one day He is going to end all of that and bring prosperity to His people. But we don't have to wait to work for justice in this area, right now—today—there are more than enough ways we can pursue economic justice for all people and work to bring peace.

Message Point 3: "Peace Comes with Truth-Telling" (vv. 14–17)

Zechariah also brings up the matter of truth telling. A lot of times, we don't tell the truth in order to keep the peace, but Zechariah is saying God requires us to tell the truth. This especially goes for the court system where lies are being told. Criminals are getting away scot-free, and innocent people are being sentenced and exploited. In this era of fake news, the world of politics needs truth-telling, and as Christians, we must be examples in this area.

THAT'LL PREACH

Whenever there's a leak, our first thought is to grab a bucket or a towel to make sure the water doesn't damage where it's landing. This can only last for so long. We will always hear the sound of the water dripping into the bucket. We will always see the soaked towel in the corner. It's going to take a little more work to actually fix the leak. It's the same way when it comes to justice. A quick fix stops some damage, but it's just going to keep getting worse if we stop there. We have to get to the source of the problem to find lasting peace.

CONCLUSION

We can all see the problems around us. They stem from a lack of justice, and a lack of justice leads to a lack of peace. The world seeks peace, but it can only come through justice. It's going to take God's people to usher in God's justice so the world can know God's peace.

NOTES

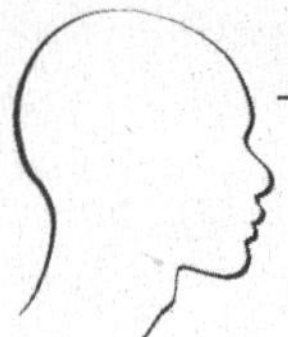

Temporary Fix

By Rev. Cheryl Price

Lesson Theme	Unit Theme	Scripture
Practice Justice	Called to God's Work of Justice	Jeremiah 21:8–14

INTRODUCTION

Our actions have consequences. Jeremiah had prophesied Jerusalem's destruction. Unfortunately, to the demise of the city leaders, they had chosen to deny Jeremiah's prophecy from the Lord. King Zedekiah realized the destruction of Jerusalem by King Nebuchadnezzar needed intervention from the Lord. He sent the prophet Pashur and the priest Zephaniah to inquire of how God could deliver them from Nebuchadnezzar. Zedekiah needed God's help, but he neither acknowledged God when Jeremiah proclaimed Jerusalem's demise nor did he repent of his sin. Zedekiah thought of God as a temporary fix to his immediate battles. But he was unwilling to have a permanent and authentic relationship with the Lord.

MESSAGE POINTS

Message Point 1: "Choose Life or Death" (Jeremiah 21:8–10)
Nebuchadnezzar is attacking the city, and there is no help from the Lord. In fact, Jeremiah tells Pashur and the priest Zephaniah to tell the people to decide if they want to live or die. The people in Jerusalem can surrender or choose to stay in the city. If they surrender, they will be held as captives and live in Babylon as exiles. Or they can die from famine, a plague, or the sword. Which would they decide? Fight for a losing cause or go willingly to an unknown land with customs, beliefs, and traditions that are not completely theirs? God states emphatically that Jerusalem will not be saved. If the leadership, including Zedekiah, had shown how to live with justice and care for the people, the situation would not be so horrible. What does this say about the roles of leaders and whom people choose to follow? Choosing what God wants for our lives may require us to do what we would rather not do. We often seek temporary pleasure or unjust actions over God's justice and ways. In the end, when we choose life in the Lord, we choose an everlasting promise that will guide us and keep us

Message Point 2: "God's Wrath and Evil Leaders" (vv. 11–12)
Verses 11 and 12 clearly articulate the Lord's disgust with the city leaders. King Zedekiah, his administrators, and various other leaders will not escape the punishment God has for them because of their oppressive behavior and unjust ways. If there is no change from their injustice, God will respond. The Lord's response to their evil ways will burn like fire, and nothing and no one will be able to extinguish it. Zedekiah and his leaders were evil and showed no signs of repentance. They did not fear God and created an environment where evil could prosper. Zedekiah and his leaders are reminders that leaders must be careful to create relationships and systems that encourage and foster healthy, just opportunities for everyone's benefit. Although evil and unjust leaders continue to thrive and rule, Jeremiah reminds us that God expects more from leaders, and we should too. How will evil

leaders experience God's wrath, and how will believers stand up against oppression? Take a stand and choose to do what is right before God.

Message Point 3: Punishment Deserved (vv. 13–14)

Their lack of repentance, compassion, and mercy for the people is intentionally reflected in how the Lord will destroy the leaders and the people of Jerusalem. The location of Jerusalem, surrounded by valleys and nestled on a rocky plateau, gave false hope to the city's inhabitants. Jeremiah declares the Lord has said the leaders who do not change from their oppressive and evil ways will experience a fire that will destroy everything they own. The fire will destroy and cleanse the area. What the leaders hold to be honorable and worthy of their praise will be destroyed. God's punishment is what they deserve for their lack of justice.

THAT'LL PREACH

Once there was a delicate bridge that was getting worn down from people walking across it and digging their sharp heels, spikes, and tools into its fine wood. It was initially made for sandals and tennis shoes to grace its brown wood. Eventually, the bridge's builder noticed the wood was becoming worn and thought, "Why can't they walk softer or put a covering across my fine bridge? It would be helpful if they warned the people with the spiked heels, sharp tools, and other pointy objects not to cross the bridge unless they covered the pointy objects." The first few days things worked out fine, but as the week went on, people either forgot or did not think it was necessary. Eventually, the bridge could not take the pressure, and it became weaker. The bridge builder posted another sign that warned if the pointy and spiky items were not covered, no one would be allowed to cross the bridge. After another week, the people would not stop crossing with spikes. Finally the bridge gave in and was destroyed. People protested, but the bridge builder would not rebuild the bridge. If only they had followed the bridge builder's rules before it was too late.

CONCLUSION

There are consequences to disobeying God. Although we prefer to discuss and experience God without judgment or punishment, this does not happen. Our actions will bring consequences now or later. Will we decide to obey today? We can have nice, pretty things, but we must not make these things our gods to worship. We cannot make nice things the focus of who we are becoming. God is not a temporary fix but an invitation for a permanent relationship of loving, following, and doing justice.

NOTES

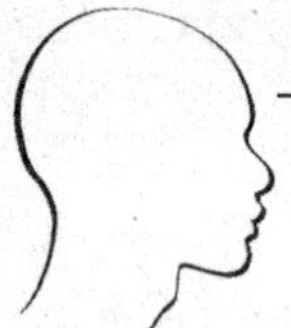

Evil Kings, Beware!

By Rev. Cheryl Price, PhD

Lesson Theme	Unit Theme	Scripture
Repent of Injustice	Called to God's Work of Justice	Jeremiah 22:1–10

INTRODUCTION

Doing justice and living just lives are requirements and expectations God has embedded in the very foundation of the kingdom of God. The kings and the people of God were to live their lives in just and merciful ways. Yet the kings oppressed the people. God sent a warning through Jeremiah to the kings to repent of their sins and to implement justice in their policies and practices. If the kings did not change their evil ways, God would bring His wrath and destruction upon the king and the people.

MESSAGE POINTS

Message Point 1: "Justice Requires Hospitality and Unselfishness" (Jeremiah 22:1–5)
Jeremiah identifies God's standards of justice, love, and care that King Jehoiakim and future kings are to follow. The king should (1) turn from evil and do what is right; (2) treat the stranger, the fatherless, and the widow with respect and care for them; and (3) stop placing burdens of the people through taxes and hard labor with no pay. The king needed to repent inwardly and outwardly to make a change. What does this mean to us? We too must repent of our selfishness and live in just ways. We are not to treat justice as an open invitation we receive from God. We cannot decide to RSVP with regrets when we would rather not feed the homeless or are too busy to stop and help someone in need. Take action that is truly from the heart and that can assist someone. Be careful not to build a name for yourself at the expense of not caring for others. In verse 5, God declares to the king that if repentance and changes do not happen, the palace will be destroyed. The Lord has given the king a choice. What choice will you make? To paraphrase what Micah 6:8 (KJV) asks, "What does God require of each of us, but to do justice and walk humbly before our God?" Let our walking shoes display hospitality with the goal of justice as its soles.

Message Point 2: "Beauty Becomes Ashes" (vv. 6–9)
Jeremiah gives details about the destruction of the palace if the orphan, the widows, and the strangers are not shown the proper hospitality and love. It's amazing how God targeted what King Jehoiakim really loved the most: his beautiful palace. The glorious palace with its fine cedar beams will be cut and thrown into the fire and be burnt up like cheap wood, with no value (v. 6). King Jehoiakim valued a beautiful building and the admiration of others over the welfare of people. People will ask why the palace and the city were destroyed. The answer will be they did not follow the covenant of the Lord and they worshiped other gods (vv. 8–9). Obedience and only worshiping the one and only true God are prerequisites. Check who you are worshiping and obeying. Do you live to watch the lives of celebrities or your friends at the expense of defining who you really are in the Lord? Beauty in our eyes can become ashes that will crumble and turn to dust that God's breath of life will not resurrect.

Message Point 3: "Point of No Return" (v. 10)

The people cried over the death of King Josiah at the battle of Megiddo. Josiah was a good king, and his son Shallum became the king for only three months after his father's death. King Shallum was dethroned and taken into exile by Egypt. He would never return to the throne. Mourning for the way things were with King Josiah would not help to bring a change. King Shallum's exile should have been a clear warning that things were changing and that the king and the people needed to make a change. Unfortunately crying over the past and not facing their present reality was a waste of tears. The people, the king, and future kings needed to wake up to their new reality. Repent, obey, and worship the living God. That would change their lives. We too must repent, obey, and worship God.

THAT'LL PREACH

On a cold and windy day, a boy huddled in a box. He had wrapped his chest and legs in a large plastic bag to keep warm inside the box. He hoped maybe one of the people walking by would see him. If they saw him, then just maybe, one of them would stop and offer him something warm to drink or give him a few dollars to buy some food. As people hurried by, no one stopped. A few people would glance his way, but no one stopped. He wondered if any of them were Christians. After about two hours, a man stopped and asked him if he was okay. The man gave him a jacket and shared that he had just left a shelter. The man cared enough to show mercy and care. This was a test to see if anyone would assist the boy. Whom did you pass by today that you could have or should have helped?

CONCLUSION

Unrighteousness, injustice, and evil are unacceptable to God even when they look good and feel better. A change has to happen. Will the kings change or stay the course of selfishness, injustice, and wicked behavior? God's wrath will be felt. But the love and justice of God lives on and is experienced by many people in many ways. Remember, God loves justice and expects believers to keep justice alive in our everyday acts of kindness, hospitality, and fighting for just systems in all walks of life. Be a defender of justice—God's justice!

NOTES

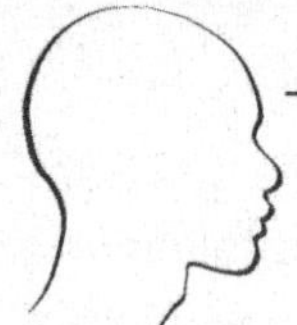

Return to God Again

By Porsha Williams

Lesson Theme	Unit Theme	Scripture
Return to Love and Justice	Called to God's Work of Justice	Hosea 11:1–2, 7–10; 12:1–2, 6–14

INTRODUCTION

The relationship between God and the Children of Israel can be seen as a relationship that is constantly in flux. One day, Israel is in good graces. The next, God is seeking to pursue wrath. Even still, there is a desire to be close at all costs. In the book of Hosea, specifically, we see this relationship portrayed as a marriage where Israel is an unfaithful wife. Israel has turned her heart away from God, and she decided to do her own thing without any regard for her husband. Israel and God's relationship is also depicted as a child to parent, which is a common relationship seen throughout the biblical text. In our passage of Scripture for today, witnessing the ebbs and flows of God's relationship with the Children of Israel is no different. The strain between God and Israel is ongoing, still, there is good news.

MESSAGE POINTS

Message Point 1: "Israel Turns Away from God, Again" (Hosea 11:1–2)

God loves all of His children. There is no secret about that. Israel, the chosen people, were called out of Egypt because God loved them so much. Israel was once abused by the oppressive systems of Egypt, and God called them to be delivered from Egypt, as we witness in the book of Exodus. Yet, even though Israel was rescued from the hands of its enemy, Israel turned its heart away from God and began to worship and make sacrifices to other gods. The more that God called to the Israelites, the more they turned away from Him (Hosea 11:2). The Israelites began making sacrifices to Baalim and burned incense to images (v. 2). This behavior is offensive to God because God made it clear that the Israelites should not worship or serve any other gods besides Him. Yet, again, they have turned. As a result, God decides that He will no longer exalt them above any other race of people (v. 7).

Message Point 2: "God Has Compassion" (vv. 7–10)

Even though the Israelites turn away from God intentionally, somehow God is compassionate and loving toward them. God asks the question, "How shall I ...," which signals that God is pondering and showing compassion (Hosea 11:8). God has a heart for His greatest love to return. Even when the people are abusive in actions and unfaithful to God, God still manages to think about His love first. God continuously starts and ends with love. God's heart is changed through the power of love. God's forgivingness comes from love. These things remind us that love is full of saving power. God has a plan to evoke fear and anger, but God said that He will not do these things (Hosea 11:9). Love is the reason God is able to be kind and just. That is how we too are called to be. We are called to have a justice that is rooted in love. For with love, God shares that the people will eventually return to God and follow Him. When God speaks and roars, His children will return to Him once more.

Message Point 3: "Return to God" (Hosea 12:6–14)

In order to maintain love and justice, one must return to God. Returning to God, who is the source of love and justice, must be at the center. Ephraim, specifically, has been dishonest and unjust to the point of cheating and disenfranchising other people. That is not the way of God. Not only has Israel turned away from God, but Ephraim has also been unjust and decided to get rich off of the less fortunate. This portion of Scripture is a plea and a judgment that should push the people back to God. Without God, what could anyone do? God desires to be close, yet people must choose God for themselves. If the people decide not to turn to God, He will send forth a punishment. It is clear that God is angry though still compassionate. God is willing to save when the people turn from their wicked ways and come back to Him.

THAT'LL PREACH

Teenage years are some of the most important years in human development. The stage of being a young child who depends on their parents moves toward a more independent state. Temper tantrums and crying spells lessen, and responsibility and rebellion tend to increase. Teenagers tend to find themselves doing what they want without any explanation, and the fear of consequence is decreased. Parents still have a set of rules and guidelines, yet teens tend to disobey. For instance, curfew. Almost every teenager will break curfew, which is a set time that a teen is required to be home. In many instances, curfew is broken because of deliberate decisions and distractions. The children of God in this text have shown their teenage tendencies. They have turned away from God and have become distracted and have made deliberate decisions that have led to divine disappointment. While compassionate, God's disappointment is seen in this text. God desires better for His children and hopes that His children will make wise decisions regarding justice.

CONCLUSION

In conclusion, the children of God had turned away from God once again. They turned to other gods and made sacrifices to those other gods. Even in their disobedience and their turning away, God desired to be close to the people. God is willing to be compassionate and loving. God is also willing to be just by any means necessary. However, at some point, the people of God need to return to Him, for if not, God will be sure to cut them off and bring judgment. God is willing to relent once the people turn to Him.

NOTES

____

____

____

____

____

____

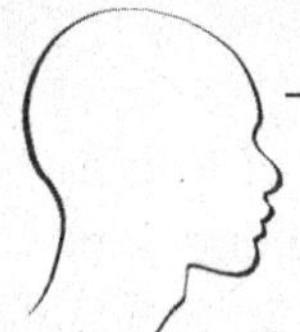

Living in the Rhythm of Wisdom

By Dr. R. Neal Siler

Lesson Theme	Unit Theme	Scripture
The Call of Wisdom	Wisdom in Proverbs	Proverbs 1:1–4, 7–8, 10–11, 20–22, 32–33

INTRODUCTION

In *Anam Cara: A Book of Celtic Wisdom,* author John Donohue writes, "Wisdom is the art of balancing the known with the unknown, the suffering with the joy; it is a way of linking the whole of life together in a new and deeper unity ... Wisdom is the art of living in rhythm with your soul, your life, and the divine." The idea of living in such a life's rhythm sounds wonderful. It is a way of living in deep awareness of what brings one's soul the deepest satisfaction. Such a rhythm proposes that one is living life on purpose—respectful of God's desires, self, and others—but also respectful of what pleases God. This is a grand and lofty aspiration, but the text clarifies for us that without knowledge and understanding, living in such a rhythm will be next to impossible. Yet, I believe God wants us to honor Him by deeply connecting with Him in our soul such that our outward life will reflect this vibrant rhythm.

MESSAGE POINTS

Message Point 1: "Wisdom Is a Journey of Knowledge and Instruction" (Proverbs 1:1–4, 7–8)

We do not become wise overnight. Wisdom is a journey. In this journey, we discover what is out of balance. We also begin to get a sense of the non-negotiables that will ensure that we can balance the known with the unknown and the suffering with the joy in a way that links the whole of our lives together in a deeper unity. The writer of Proverbs reminds us, "The fear of the LORD is the beginning of knowledge: but fools despise wisdom and instruction" (Proverbs 1:7). Wisdom starts with knowledge, but the fear of the Lord is the landscape of the journey. The fear of the Lord involves awe, reverence, love, and trust in God, and it must come first. But you must also take instruction. Learn all you can from godly people; they are the voice of the Lord when you find yourself in a wilderness. If you will do this, wisdom gives honor, guidance, and protection.

Message Point 2: "The Rhythm of Wisdom Is Understanding in Practice" (vv. 10–11, 20–22)

In truth, a person can have wisdom but have no understanding of how to appropriate what has been taught or learned. But because not everyone lives in a place of truth and goodness, it pays to practice what you understand. This will help us recognize those who live in hostility to truth and good and how this breaks the peace. These are those who call us to harass the innocent (v. 11). When we aspire to live in a place of peace and goodness but others thwart our efforts, this is when understanding becomes wisdom's greatest ally. There are many reasons this may be the case. Chiefly, we do not know what barriers and hindrances another person carries with them that makes it so difficult for them to live the joys of life. If a person lacks understanding, or they themselves feel misunderstood, they may not be able to act wisely in situations that require wisdom. There is no better dividend for discovering how to live in wisdom's rhythm.

Message Point 3: "Wisdom Is the Art of Perceiving Truth, Right, and Wrong" (vv. 32-33)
But it is not just about wisdom, which is knowledge of what is true and moral, but also understanding of that wisdom. Understanding is the ability to perceive and discern a situation in order to apply wisdom. Understanding is the gift of discernment. It provides an internal barometer for perceiving truth and for knowing the difference between right and wrong. There is much security in knowing that you are doing the right thing. Living in the rhythm of wisdom, you are alert to the abuses and injuries that can come from not knowing. Understanding helps steer one away from outcomes that can injure or depart from situations that may cause harm. Looking at Proverbs 1:32–33 a stern warning is followed by a powerful admonition. The warning is against waywardness, which can be either turning away from what is right or proper, or complacency, which is a feeling of smug or uncritical satisfaction with oneself or one's achievements. This is followed by a powerful admonition that "whoso hearkeneth unto [wisdom] shall dwell safely, and shall be quiet from fear of evil."

THAT'LL PREACH

I love James 1:5: "If any of you lack wisdom, let him ask of God, that giveth to all men liberally, and upbraideth not; and it shall be given him."

Therefore, wisdom is the principal thing, along with understanding. Wisdom is incomplete without understanding. Every experience takes us further into the throes of wisdom and understanding if we will open ourselves to these lessons. Perhaps you have found yourself in a place where wisdom and understanding failed you. Proverbs 21:30 tell us, "There is no wisdom nor understanding nor counsel against the LORD." Maybe this is wisdom's invitation to you. Have you stood on your wisdom? Is it not God's wisdom that you desire? That is the only wisdom that can stand in the face of the wisdom of man, which is at best limited and filled with selfish expectations. True wisdom, as all truth, rests in God's love toward us, and His demonstration of that love in sacrificing His one and only Son, Jesus.

CONCLUSION

Sometimes life can get in the way and we feel we're just not ready to handle the full impact of God's wisdom, much less how we can invest in God's wisdom for ourselves. Sometimes we aren't prepared to use it, and sometimes we're not mature enough. But discovering the rhythm of wisdom is a great journey, and when the Lord gives us understanding, we can appropriate His wisdom in all things. The key is we must wait, be patient, and have faith. Even the saints of the early church had to learn this lesson. Learning to live in the rhythm of wisdom will help you turn away when your choices and decisions may take you to an unwise place. As we practice living in the rhythm of wisdom, we grow in the gifts of grace, patience, and faithfulness—the fruit that flows from the life of the wise.

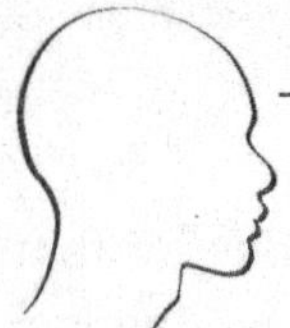

The Treasure of Wisdom

By Dr. Rev. Matthew C. Jones

Lesson Theme	Unit Theme	Scripture
The Value of Wisdom	Wisdom in Proverbs	Proverbs 2:1–11

INTRODUCTION

If you want to grow in wisdom, read the book of Proverbs. It is a storehouse of wisdom teachings. The word *wisdom* itself is mentioned over one hundred times in the book. The major author of the book was a man renowned for his wisdom, Solomon, the ancient King of Israel who was given supernatural wisdom from God (1 Kings 4:29). Along with Solomon, the book includes more wise people, like the men of Hezekiah (25:1), Agur (30:1), King Lemuel's mother (31:1), as well as some anonymous wise folks (22:17). In the second chapter of Proverbs, we see Solomon urging his son in the way of wisdom, instructing him to treasure it in the same way a wealthy man treasures his riches, acknowledging true wealth is found in God alone. Let's discuss these themes, as we get into the text of Proverbs chapter 2.

MESSAGE POINTS

Message Point 1: "Treasuring Wisdom" (Proverbs 2:1–4)

In the opening four verses of the second chapter of Proverbs, we see wisdom described as a treasure and compared to "silver" (v. 4), and not just any old treasure or precious silver, but a "hidden" one. This means it must be sought after if it is to be found. And when wisdom is discovered, the treasure hunter is supposed to treasure that treasure. The redundancy here in my wording is important for it reflects the text, which speaks of treasure as a verb in verse 1 to pursue ("treasure my commandments") and then as a noun in verse 4, to be cherished. The treasure is wisdom, which these verses tie to the Torah, specifically to understanding in one's heart of God's will (v. 2) and obeying His commandments (v. 1).

Message Point 2: "Tearful Worship" (vv. 5–8)

Unlike knowledge, which is something we can memorize, wisdom comes from our experiences with obeying God and maturing in him. Biblical wisdom is not just life experience though; it is growing in a reverent and passionate worship of God in the world. In the fifth verse, we read of the fear of the Lord, which is an important component of worship. According to Proverbs 9:10, "The fear of the LORD is the beginning of wisdom." It begins with the worshiper before the triune God, for He is the fountain and dispenser of true wisdom. In verse six, we read about how "the LORD giveth wisdom." In fact, God "layeth up sound wisdom" (v. 7) and gives it to His children as they seek Him. The text describes these worshipers as "them that walk uprightly" (v. 7). As a community of faithful worshipers, God's people are not merely on a quest for wisdom, but more importantly, they are in pursuit of the One who gives it.

Message Point 3: "True Wealth" (vv. 9–11)

As the Lord gives wisdom to His people, they discover true wealth. Their eyes become sensitive to "understand righteousness, and judgment" (v. 9). The wise person is described as being committed to others, seeking "equity" and "every good path" (v. 9). From this we see how wisdom in practice provides a deep well of moral discernment in one's "heart" that is "pleasant unto thy soul" (v. 10). Unlike other things in this world we chase after, which often leave us feeling empty, wisdom truly satisfies the worshiper of God. Along with satisfying us, wisdom is protective. Verse eleven promises it will guard and watch over us. The protection wisdom offers us comes as it keeps us away from the dangers and consequences of sinful living. In Scripture, wisdom is not mere intellectual understanding; rather, it is moral know-how and a commitment of the will to joyfully obey the Lord in the face of our fallen world.

THAT'LL PREACH

In 1 Corinthians, the Apostle Paul writes to the ancient church in Corinth about the wisdom of God and juxtaposes it with the world (1:19–2:16). As he opens the letter, Paul rhetorically exposes worldly wisdom and taunts, "Where is the wise?" (1:20) He warns that the wisdom of the age does not lead to God (1:21) and goes on to explain how the gospel of Jesus is seen as foolishness to the world (1:21–24). This comes as no surprise, for as Psalm 14:1 says, "The fool hath said in his heart, There is no God. They are corrupt, they have done abominable works, there is none that doeth good." Blinded by sin, the world sees God and his wisdom revealed in Christ as foolish (1:24–25), which Paul uses to remind believers of our calling (1:26–30). As Paul explains our salvation by grace, he urges his readers to "glory in the Lord" (1:31) and continue in the mission of the Gospel with God's strength and wisdom (2:1–16). Apart from Christ's work and the Spirit's power, we would be separated from not only the wisdom of the Father, but also His love. As we read Proverbs 2 and think about receiving wisdom from God in our lives, let us rejoice in the reality that in salvation we have "Christ the power of God, and the wisdom of God" (1:24). He is our ultimate treasure to be treasured above all things in this world.

CONCLUSION

In our study of Proverbs 2, we were invited to seek and find the treasure of wisdom. The verses we explored had a series of conditional statements, reminding us the pursuit of wisdom requires action. Verses 3 and 4 both begin by saying, "If you ..." Similarly, James 1:5 begins with an "if" while also talking about the pursuit of wisdom ("If any of you lack wisdom, let him ask of God ..."). In response to learning about wisdom, we need to make sure we don't leave our study with the conditional "if," and instead let's move to action right now. Scripture is clear that wisdom doesn't just happen; it comes as we pursue and obey God (cf. Ephesians 5:15–18). In teaching His disciples about wisdom, Jesus spoke about a wise man who built his home on a solid foundation versus the foolish man who builds on shifting sand (Matthew 7:24–29). The Lord drove home the importance of obedient action in response to His teaching, saying, "Therefore whosoever heareth these sayings of mine, and doeth them, I will liken him unto a wise man, which built his house upon a rock" (v. 24). May the tender mercies of the Lord move us now to act upon His words and in works of righteousness by His sanctifying power for His name's sake. Amen.

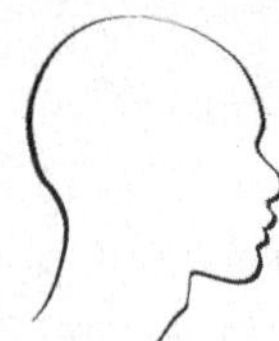

The Guiding Light of Wisdom

By Pastor Tommy E. Smith, Jr.

Lesson Theme	Unit Theme	Scripture
The Gifts of Wisdom	Wisdom in Proverbs	Proverbs 8:8–14, 17–21

INTRODUCTION

What is most important for humans to possess if they wish to live the most productive life possible? This question is something King Solomon spent much of his life pursuing, and he spared no expense in using his considerable wealth and privilege to answer it. What he came up with is worth our attention too. Solomon concluded that wisdom is the trait that will best ensure a successful outcome in life. This is because wisdom begins with the fear of the Lord, and that perspective governs the application and use of all other knowledge we acquire. Solomon was so moved by this realization that he made every effort to convey this information to his children, Israel's future leaders, and eventually all who would seek to live in fellowship with God. There are many reasons that God so highly values wisdom. Today we will look briefly at three of them: wisdom's attributes, its work, and its benefits.

MESSAGE POINTS

Message Point 1: "The Attributes of Wisdom" (Proverbs 8:8–12)

Solomon has great regard for wisdom, and to help convey this to his hearers he uses the literary device of personifying wisdom as a virtuous woman. Wisdom and knowledge are closely related, and sometimes thought of as synonyms. However, the two are different. Knowledge is the accumulation of information, while wisdom is the ability to use knowledge to its fullest extent. Among the attributes, Solomon lists for wisdom is an absolute purity that does not contain a hint of perverseness. Instead, what wisdom does possess is understanding, insight, and the ability to anticipate and act accordingly (prudence). Wisdom has no tolerance for evil, for wisdom realizes that the fear of the Lord begins with her! For this reason, she is better than gold, silver, precious stones, and all of the other material possessions that humanity places so much value on. Because wisdom can have such a profound impact on the direction of a person's life, Solomon feels a particular urgency for it to be possessed in one's youth.

Message Point 2: "The Work of Wisdom" (vv. 13–14)

Wisdom exists for a reason and has a task to perform. Wisdom allows us to make sense of the world. Our five senses are a constant source of stimulation and information. This near-continuous flow of data into our brains must be organized and categorized in order for it to be useful for us. The brain has a marvelous capability to process and analyze this information, in many ways more powerful than today's most advanced supercomputers. Yet this processing power alone is not enough to navigate us through life. Life's most important questions and decisions require a higher level of reasoning and analysis than the brain alone can provide. What we need to be successful in life from God's perspective is wisdom. Wisdom lets us know what attitudes are right, what actions should be shunned, and how to gain God's favor. Solomon may not have known much about neurotransmitters, but he knew that dedication to God and a commitment to righteousness give us an insight in life that will ultimately draw us closer to the very heart of God, through wisdom!

Message Point 3: "The Benefits of Wisdom" (vv. 17–21)

The person who lives a life rich in wisdom is someone who is abundantly blessed with the goodness and favor that this life has to offer. Wisdom has tremendous and unique benefits for those who possess her. Solomon describes these as including riches, honor, and righteousness. This suggests material sufficiency, mental stability, and moral certainty. Considering how much effort is expended in our society by individuals in pursuit of each of these feelings, those who possess wisdom are favored indeed. For this reason, Solomon characterizes wisdom's value as being better than even fine gold and choice silver. In being led by wisdom, we are equipped to walk in pathways that are pleasing to God. A mental image arising from Solomon's words is that of a soldier walking through a minefield. There are so many ways to make a wrong step, and without x-ray vision, the task can seem impossibly hopeless. Wisdom's value is that it gives this soldier the essential "below the surface" information necessary to ensure safe passage through this dangerous terrain!

THAT'LL PREACH

The science fiction writer Isaac Asimov once remarked, "The saddest aspect of life right now is that science gathers knowledge faster than society gathers wisdom." These words are unfortunately quite true and are similar to those spoken by Dr. Martin Luther King Jr. when he said, "We have allowed our civilization to outrun our culture, and so we are in danger now of ending up with guided missiles in the hands of misguided men." What King and Asimov both realized is that it takes wisdom to exercise appropriate rule over knowledge. Our knowledge today has shown us how to unleash the destruction of hell by splitting atoms and how to engineer microbes that our immune systems may not even know how to fight. Soon a world power could deploy these technologies in a manner that fails to appreciate all of the possible disastrous and even global consequences. For this reason, wisdom has never been more important. Yet, as these two men (and Solomon) have implied, our commitment to wisdom as a society may not be up to the task. For this reason, it is vitally important that believers strive to seek wisdom early and embrace it throughout our lives!

CONCLUSION

As has been verified time and time again, the ancient writings of Scripture have proven to offer the most up-to-date and accurate guidance for addressing humanity's most pressing problems. While God uses instincts to direct the actions of animals, humans are given the privilege of ordering their lives based on knowledge. God has given humanity formidable mental and intellectual tools for acquiring knowledge. However, without the guiding oversight of wisdom, our knowledge can be a source of misery and pain. To slightly paraphrase Dr. King: Wisdom can transform our discordant lives into a beautiful symphony of godliness, peace, and love—for God and one another!

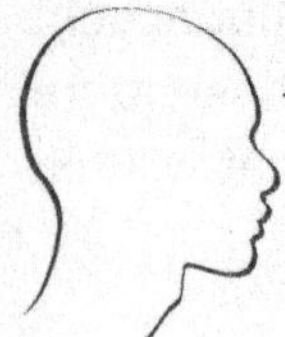

JUNE 28, 2020

The Nourishment of Wisdom

By Howard Lee Thomas III

Lesson Theme	Unit Theme	Scripture
Wisdom's Feast	Wisdom in Proverbs	Proverbs 9:1–6, 8–10, 13–18

INTRODUCTION

Solomon did not write all of the proverbs in the book of Proverbs, but he was known to have written or inspired the production of thousands of proverbs. This is mainly due to the rich blessing that God gave Solomon of wisdom and the ability to apply wisdom to everyday living. Because of this reputation, proverbs written after him or during his time were often attributed to him in order to forward his reputation and example. Proverbs 1:8–9:18 represents a specific cycle of two temptations that can lure one away from a blessed life: first, wealth through dishonest gain, and second, pleasure found outside of the God-willed confines and commitments of marriage. Chapter 9, our passage for today, focuses on the trappings of pleasure outside of marriage. Overall, Solomon's thesis for a good life is one who seeks to fear God's power first and thus revere His instructions and ways. False wisdom is that which does not fear and respect God as a foundation. This sermon emphasizes that true wisdom comes from biblical foundations ultimately displayed in Jesus Christ as the way to keep from being seduced to fall into worldly destruction.

MESSAGE POINTS

Message Point 1: "Wisdom Has Set Her House" (Proverbs 9:1–6)

"Wisdom has set her house" is the tone setter for this sermon because it communicates that wisdom is here, and wisdom is established, strong, legitimate, and not going anywhere. This fact also then establishes that if you do not respect this establishment, then you will be crushed by it via the consequences. Respecting the power and blessing of wisdom is the focus of Psalm 9:1–6. Also, there is a intimate, nourishing, and mothering tone to the passages. "Come in with me" and "come eat my food" are both images meant to convey that full desire (emotional, mental, physical) is necessary to pursue wisdom correctly, and that God's wisdom desires our entire being to be blessed beyond what can be measured and beyond what the world could promise. Also, there is an evangelistic tone to verses 1 through 6. This emphasizes that wisdom desires us to desire her and that we have no excuse to miss the invitation if we are really looking. We must respect wisdom and are called to desire wisdom strongly.

Message Point 2: "Don't Waste Your Time" (vv. 8–10)

It is of essential importance to desire wisdom with all of yourself, since she calls out and knows what is best for us. Those who do not desire wisdom are fools and will lead you to foolishness if you give them your time. Basically, fools do not notice a good thing when it is calling to them and thus choose evil instead. If you try to speak wisdom to fools, they will not notice since they do not desire what is good. Some examples of foolishness are:

choosing to not exercise, eating unhealthy foods, choosing to not listen to the wise, binging on Netflix, arguing with people on social media comment sections, not listening, not fully committing to your marital relationship forever, not being humble and learning from others, refusing to submit to the Gospel of Jesus, not trusting God with your income, and so on. The focus of good wisdom is that God has made us and thus knows what is best for us, the foolish do not consume what is best and thus incur consequences instead of blessings.

Message Point 3: "Foolishness Mimics Wisdom" (vv. 13–18)

There is a "mirror" to Lady Wisdom in Lady Folly. The image of a woman at a door calling out with "come in with me" is used again to show a mimic/mirror deception to wisdom but the result is far different (v. 18). The earnings of sin are death, but the gift of God is eternal life. The two choices are before us like two paths staring us in the face: wisdom or folly. Most of what befalls us is due to this choice, and the motivation to make that choice is usually a desire that is rooted in a relationship. Folly mimics the passion and call to Wisdom, but the difference is that Folly does not root herself in the fear of God nor does she desire His ways and Words. Do relationships lead us to the intersection of how to choose life or death, Wisdom or Folly. Moreover, we can be lured one way or another based on which one we desire. Our relationship with Jesus is the guide to choosing well. Do you have an ongoing relationship with Jesus in order to be guided to the right direction of life?

THAT'LL PREACH

Jesus said to His disciples, "I will make you fishers of men" (Matthew 4:19). I have only been fishing once, mainly because when I went, it was a terrible experience. I only caught one small fish, and it took a lot of strategy and patience to catch it. One factor in why I did not catch many fish was the lure; it was cheap, and fish are not attracted to cheap lures. A good fisherman has an attractive lure and knows how to entice fish to come to it. God and Satan are good fishermen. But God lures us to life while Satan lures us to death. What lure are you attracted to? Often shiny and smooth-talking "lures" lead to death, but those who speak the truth, even truth that hurts, lead to life. Either way, being caught by a lure will hurt because the good things still require sacrifice and pain, but only one "lure" leads to life everlasting. Invest in the right lure, in a daily walk with Jesus, to not be caught by Folly.

CONCLUSION

The good life is being caught by the right lure—the lure of life instead of the lure of death. "Which lure are you seeking?" is the ultimate question of this sermon. Christians ought to display how the wisdom of God in Jesus is not just a type of wisdom among all the other religions, but *the* wisdom because He knows us, made us, desires us, and calls us to worship Him. Being caught by a lure will hurt, but Christ's lure of wisdom leads to a life full of lasting deep growth, strength, eternal life, and eternal blessing.

Vindication of Wisdom in the Wilderness

By Dr. Rev. Matthew C. Jones

Lesson Theme	Unit Theme	Scripture
Wisdom's Vindication	Wisdom in the Gospels	Matthew 11:7–19

INTRODUCTION

The historic prophet John the Baptist was known for his wilderness ministry. Mind you, the wilderness was not a pretty place. In the Bible, it is associated with danger and death (cf. Deuteronomy 8:15, Exodus 14:11). For example, in the tragic story of Job, the wind that ruins his house and kills his children comes from the wilderness (Job 1:19). Along with such darkness, the wilderness is a place of rebellion and punishment (cf. Numbers 14:32-33, 27:14). With these negative images in front of us, we can see the power of God coming to His people in the wilderness—of all places—to reveal Himself in the covenant at the Horeb (Exodus 3) and the Sinai (Exodus 19). This is exactly what was happening through the prophet John—he was revealing the God of the covenant to the people. Specifically, he was preparing the way for the people to see God face-to-face in the historic Jesus of Nazareth, the eternal Son incarnate. John publicly revealed Jesus in the wilderness to the people, and then our Savior went into the wasteland alone to confront Satan and the kingdom of darkness (Matthew 4:1). Thereafter, Jesus began His preaching ministry, which exposed the darkness and challenged those who rejected John's offer of repentance to prepare the way for our Lord. In Matthew 11, we see Jesus vindicating John's ministry as the very wisdom of God in the face of his rejectors.

MESSAGE POINTS

Message Point 1: "Prophecy and the Wilderness" (Matthew 11:7–10)

In verses 7 and 8, Jesus gets rather witty exposing the critics of John. Knowing the people went out to see prophet John in his rough clothes in the dry wilderness, Jesus rhetorically asks if they went out to see a "reed shaken with the wind" (v. 7) or a "man clothed in soft raiment" (v. 8). Of course, the people didn't go to see a silk gown or a shaking grass; they went to see the prophet John (that's why it's witty or sarcastic even). In the next verse (v. 9), Jesus declares John was one who is "more than a prophet." He explains that John not only offers prophecies, but he is also a fulfillment of prophecy. In verse 10, Jesus quotes Exodus 23:20 and Malachi 3:1, with allusions to Isaiah 40:3, showing that John was the fulfillment of ancient prophecy tied to the coming of the long-awaited prophesied Messiah. This fulfillment paved the way for the eternal Son to enter time and space in the historic Jesus, as the fulfillment of this prophetic figure and future sovereign of God's Kingdom in the earth.

Message Point 2: "Perception and the Willing" (vv. 11–15)

In verses 11–15, Jesus challenges the perceptions of His listeners concerning John the prophet and Himself as the Messiah. He talks about their fallen wills that were unwilling to accept the truth (v. 14), juxtaposing them with those who have ears to hear what the Lord was teaching the people (v. 15). In these verses, Jesus was specifically warning them about the spiritual and political power brokers of the day who resisted John's message and Jesus as the Messiah. He challenges this hateful hegemony of "the violent" (v. 12), who were trying to take the kingdom of God "by force" (v. 12) and therein—Jesus says—"kingdom of heaven suffereth violence" (v. 12). The foolishness of such an endeavor—impotent mortals trying to take the all-powerful immortal God's Kingdom—ought to be obvious to us. Nothing will stop God or His kingdom. Further, nothing apart from the grace of God would change the heart of these violent men trying to build their own kingdom as they rejected the Prince of Peace, Jesus the Christ.

Message Point 3: "Playing and Wisdom" (vv. 16–19)

Jesus describes those rejecting Him rather sarcastically and accurately in verses 16 and 17 as spoiled children at play. He paints the image of pouting children who will neither dance to the flute nor mourn to a dirge, which is likely in reference to music at a wedding accompanied by dancing and the songs at a funeral used for mourning. These brats were ruining celebrations and commemorations. To make sure his listeners don't miss the imagery at hand, Jesus tells us who these children are in his mind. It is those who reject John as the servant of the Messiah (v.18) and Jesus as the Son of Man (v.19). Jesus puts their reasons for rejection on blast. In verse 18, He says they attacked John, who "came neither eating nor drinking." And they attacked Jesus, who they say was the opposite, that is, He "came eating and drinking." As our Lord pointed out, they neither dance when it's time nor mourn when they should. They should have fasted with John and feasted with Jesus. Their foolish behavior serves to vindicate the wisdom of God (v.19). In verse 19, Jesus personifies wisdom and explains how "her children" exposed the hegemony, alluding back to verses 2 through 6 that document the deeds of the Lord's miracles and message.

THAT'LL PREACH

A popular acronym in our culture today is "G.O.A.T." It stands for the Greatest Of All Time. In the media, we often hear folks ask about who is the "G.O.A.T." in certain fields. For example, is Mike or LeBron the G.O.A.T. of basketball? Is Biggie or Tupac the G.O.A.T. of hip-hop? Of course, whether in basketball or hip-hop, there are many other names that come to mind when we debate who is the G.O.A.T. That said, when it comes to the G.O.A.T. of the prophets, Jesus says it was John the Baptist (Matthew 11:11). And when John was asked who was the G.O.A.T. of all creation, he replied that it was Jesus (John 1:27). In fact, John's ministry is described in Scripture as a red carpet for the true G.O.A.T.—Jesus—to walk on as His grand entry. John himself said, "He [Jesus] must increase, but I must decrease. He that cometh from above is above all" (from John 3:30–31). John preached the coming of the King of God's kingdom and boldly declared it was Jesus. And unlike the earthly kings who were corrupt and comfortable in their "soft clothing" and "kings' houses" (Matthew 11:8), the true King of glory left His heavenly palace and died naked on the Cross of Calvary. He is the greatest of all time, who became the weakest of all to save us (2 Corinthians 5:21, 13:14).

CONCLUSION

In Matthew 11:7–19, Jesus vindicates God's wisdom and love in the face of fools who hate. Matthew's writing exposed the claims of the spiritual leaders of the day toward both John and Jesus. Based on Jesus' teaching, true wisdom was found in Him. Further, John's ministry was exonerated because he bore witness of Jesus, and in doing so, he was fulfilling prophecy. This fulfillment proved he was the real deal. Added to this, the power on display in Jesus' miraculous messianic deeds was proof beyond the shadow of a doubt. The greatest miracle of the Messiah, however, was not the deaf who received their hearing again, but the spiritually deaf who were graced to hear God's wisdom in Christ (11:15). In verse 11, Jesus used the Jewish idiom, "Among those born of women," which is used to contrast natural human birth (Job 14:1; 15:14; 25:4) with the supernatural birth of those born into the kingdom of heaven (John 3:1–7). John was a citizen of this kingdom; meanwhile, the haters were attacking it and him with violence. But their attacks failed and were unmasked by the face of wisdom in John and Jesus. Let us come to the words of the prophet and the work of the Prince of Peace this day, giving thanks that we were rescued from the wilderness, given ears to hear and the promise of His kingdom. Amen.

NOTES

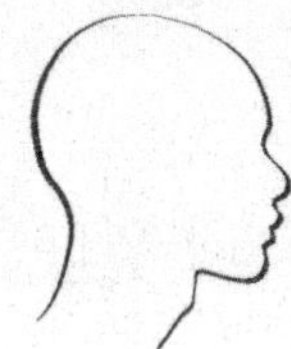

The Wisdom of a Child

By Allen Reynolds

Lesson Theme	Unit Theme	Scripture
The Boy Jesus	Wisdom in the Gospels	Ecclesiastes 3:1, 7; Luke 2:39–52

INTRODUCTION

Adults are often amazed by the wisdom of children. Not so much at their depth of revelation or ability to articulate complex teachings from the experts of the world, but by the questions they ask, the simplicity of their understanding that forces us to confront our assumptions and embrace new ways of thinking. Adults are really good at making things more complicated than they have to be. We need to decide what job to do and weigh all the pros and cons, the options, the lost time, and the impact on our reputation. A child will ask, "Which one is more fun?" We wrestle with whom we should date and what relationship to invest in until a child asks, "Are they nice? Do you like them? Are you going to get married?" Jesus challenges us with the wisdom of a child in today's lesson, reminding us we are called not to be defined by our point of departure or destination, but by our relationship with God.

MESSAGE POINTS

Message Point 1: "There's A Time for Everything" (Ecclesiastes 3:1, 7)

We live in a culture today where so much of our speech is rooted in absolutes. People love to pontificate for press and repost for likes things that they don't really fully believe. Someone will say, "I can't stand people from the other political party; they're so stupid" until they realize their boss is from that party. They refuse to speak to people who support a particular artist after a bad headline even though they were their biggest fan a few months ago. The truth is that there is a time for almost everything under the sun, and our absolutist statements are usually foolish and only half true. Ecclesiastes reminds us that everything has a time. Children should be seen and not heard, the saying goes. And people argue about it in absolute terms. When the truth is that children should be silent when a baby is sleeping but they should speak up when they need help. Wisdom knows what a situation calls for us to do.

Message Point 2: "Wisdom to Nurture" (Luke 2:39–40)

When Jesus was eight days old, He was taken to be dedicated and circumcised at the Temple, according to the Old Testament Law. His parents were faithful to honor God with their child. After he was dedicated, they went back to their hometown of Nazareth. There, Jesus grew up like a normal Jewish child His age, but it was evident that He had wisdom and the favor of God beyond His years. Sometimes when we are around children we can just see they are going to be special when they grow up. Something about how Jesus talked, how He walked, and how He lived showed that God's favor was on Him. We don't know what it was, but it was evident for all to see. And more importantly, His parents nurtured that gifting, that anointing. We would also be wise to nurture our children's gifts as well so that their lives can be used to glorify God. Where His parents lived was not what allowed them to gain glory in

God's story. But the wisdom to nurture their relationship with Jesus is what gave God glory.

Message Point 3: "When We Are Lost Being Busy" (vv. 41–52)

Mary and Joseph had gone to Jerusalem for Passover as they did each year. Jesus was almost old enough to be declared a "man" according to Jewish Law, although he was still a child under his parents' roof. Mary and Joseph had accomplished the task of worshiping God at the Temple and were journeying home to complete their trip. They were traveling with a larger group probably, but in the midst of trying to get the task done, they left behind the reason for their journey in the first place. They began to look for Jesus and found Him back at the Temple. They had just taken Jesus to participate in devotion to God. Why were they surprised that He was still back at the Temple doing just that? They had gotten so caught up in being busy, hurrying from here to there, that they forgot why they were in motion in the first place. Jesus forced them to slow down and recognize that spending time in the Heavenly Father's house was exactly where He—and they—needed to be. Yet even as the Son of God, Jesus submitted to be the son of Mary and Joseph by returning home. He was never lost because He was with His Heavenly Father. But His parents were lost until they found Jesus.

THAT'LL PREACH

The prophet Samuel was dedicated to God by his mother Hannah shortly after he was born. She had prayed for him and promised God that she would devote him to God if she was able to give birth to him. When he was young, he began to hear the voice of God and did not know it was God. He thought the high priest Eli was calling him and went to ask what he wanted. But Eli told him he had not called him. After going back and forth Eli realized what was happening and began to nurture the boy into the prophet he would become. Samuel became one of the most important prophets in Israel's history, and we know Eli pouring into him was one of the priest's greatest accomplishments in the midst of many failures. We would be wise as well to pour into the next generation because our legacies will be defined more by who remembers us than what titles hang on our wall. Relationship with God and others will always endure with more power than positions and plaques.

CONCLUSION

After Jesus returns to Nazareth at age twelve, He continues to grow in favor and wisdom as He did when He was a baby. He continued His growth into who He was destined to be. His parents continued to nurture Him, and He continued to show God's gifts in His life. I try to pray this with my young family members, that they will grow in wisdom and favor and stature with God and with people. I want to cultivate their gifts and respect God's wisdom through them, so that I may build a legacy of love that lives beyond the places I have been or things I have accomplished.

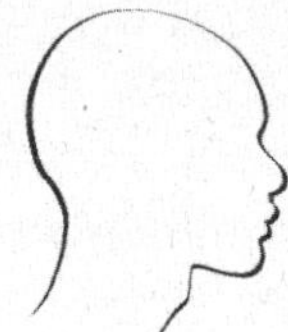

Familiarity Breeds Contempt

By Allen Reynolds, MDiv

Lesson Theme	Unit Theme	Scripture
The Wisdom of Jesus	Wisdom in the Gospels	Mark 6:1–6

INTRODUCTION

There is an old adage that familiarity breeds contempt. Sometimes the people who take us most for granted or our greatest opposition are the ones who have known us the longest or the best. It is far easier to be a fan of someone you don't have to see live in all their humanity. This was no different for Jesus, and yet He really was as great as He appeared. The people who knew Him when He was young in His hometown recognized that He was wise but out of jealousy and contempt rejected Him. They saw Him as "acting brand new" instead of recognizing He was offering brand-new life.

MESSAGE POINTS

Message Point 1: "Hometown Haters" (Mark 6:1–3)

Jesus was becoming famous throughout the region for His miraculous works. He had been healing the sick and casting out demons all across Judea and Galilee. People were showing up in crowds to hear His teaching and receive His miracles. But when He went back home, He taught at the local synagogue and got a much different reception. He was speaking as someone who had a deep revelation, authority, and power about the will of God. But the people in the audience said to themselves, "How does Jesus know so much? He went to the same school I did." "Why is He acting like He is so close to God? I was out partying with His brother last week." "Why is he talking like He's so important and has so much authority? His family works construction!" These hometown haters heard how well He spoke and the good things He was doing. They were upset because He was doing well, and they weren't. They knew Him back when he was a kid. They thought there was no way He was really the Messiah. Unfortunately, their familiarity kept them from recognizing that the Savior of the world with the power to heal and free them was standing in front of them.

Message Point 2: "The Response to Rejection" (vv. 4–6)

Jesus acknowledges the rejection of His hometown and says it is to be expected. The family and familiar often have the hardest time respecting the impact of their own members. He was called to be the greatest prophet ever, and yet those who were closest to Him in the past could not receive His words from God. He was the Word of God, and they didn't want to hear Him because they knew Him when He was a kid. He had built their furniture, so He couldn't build their futures. The wisdom of Jesus that flowed from God was being ignored because the face was too familiar. As a result, of their not trusting Jesus to be the Messiah, He could not do *many* miracles there. But He still did some miracles! Jesus was not disabled by the majority who disbelieved; He still responded to the few who did! The wisdom and wonder-working power of Jesus are available to anyone who puts their faith in Him. It does not matter what the majority says. Jesus tends to those who seek Him.

THAT'LL PREACH

There is a famous book called *The Count of Monte Cristo*. It tells the story of a wealthy man who shows up in a city seemingly out of nowhere. He shows off his great wealth with the finest clothes, lavish meals, charm, and wit that make him stand out even among the rich merchants and political elites in the city. Everyone tries to figure out who he is and how they have never heard of him. "How could this rich, powerful, brilliant man have not been known by me?" they ask themselves. Well, eventually it is revealed that he was a prisoner whom they all betrayed, robbed, and left for dead. And he has returned with great fortune that leaves them all regretting their betrayal. The Count of Monte Cristo was a former prisoner. They did not recognize him because they could not imagine the same man becoming so great.

CONCLUSION

We would be wise to hear God speaking through us no matter who the vessel is. Whether God speaks through someone famous on a platform or through a cousin we haven't heard from in years, God can use whomever God chooses. Let us not be like the people in Nazareth who refused to receive what God had for them because the messenger was too familiar. Let us humble ourselves to receive the wisdom of Jesus, even when it comes from a familiar face.

NOTES

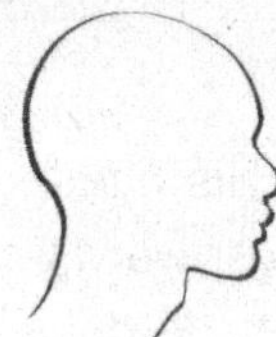

The Wise Way to True Life

By Allen Reynolds, MDiv

Lesson Theme	Unit Theme	Scripture
Wisdom: The Way, Truth, and Life	Wisdom in the Gospels	John 14:1–14

INTRODUCTION

We live in an age where there is access to more information than we could ever imagine, and certainly, more than we can manage. We have to develop advanced computer algorithms just to sort through the information to find what is relevant. We used to think that knowledge was our gateway to living our best lives. If we could only know more, we would be better. But our society is forcing us to reckon with that false assumption. We know more than ever and yet are increasingly worse off. This could be because knowledge means nothing without wisdom, the ability to apply knowledge to live life well. And wisdom does not come from information but by revelation. The greatest revelation is this: the source of all wisdom is God. In order to access this wisdom, we have been given the revelation of Jesus Christ.

MESSAGE POINTS

Message Point 1: "Jesus the Way to Comfort" (John 14:1–4)

This passage in John is one of the most profound in all of Scripture. And yet it is deeply challenging to understand. Jesus opens this chapter in the upper room speaking to His disciples. The first point He makes is about His approaching death. Science has taught us more about the process of dying than ever before. But even doctors who see it every day are still challenged by its meaning. Likewise, the disciples are challenged that Jesus will not be with them anymore physically but will be preparing a place for them. In the midst of Jesus' coming departure from the world, He gives the wisdom to comfort us all. Although He will not see us anymore in this life, He will see us in the future. When we face the death of a loved one, what we need most is not to understand why they are gone. Instead, we need the wise assurance of God that we can be comforted in their absence because they are with Him.

Message Point 2: "Jesus the Way to the Father" (vv. 5–11)

The disciples are still confused what Jesus is talking about. They don't know where He is going as He approaches His death on the Cross. They definitely don't understand that He will be resurrected and go to be with the Father. Jesus is saying they will be with Him. But they don't know how they will get there if He goes away. Jesus reveals a core theological truth for all believers. He is the way to the Father. He is one with the Father. And to the Father is where He is going. We see in Jesus the perfect representation of God. Jesus is God. It is only through Jesus revealing Himself that we have the wisdom to follow God righteously as we follow Jesus. We do not have to figure out how to get to God. There is no secret knowledge to get us to God. True wisdom is found in Jesus. But if we recognize that Jesus is God, we realize that God has come to us because we could not get to Him on our own.

Message Point 3:"Jesus the Way to Powerful Living" (vv. 12–14)

Jesus pronounces the greatest wisdom for the life of a believer with a promise: whatever we ask in His name, He will do! There is an important context to this comment, however. The ability to ask God for whatever we will, the ability to pray, is done in relationship to Jesus and accomplishing God's will. Jesus only does what He does to bring glory to God the Father. We can do greater works than Jesus did to bring glory to God. If we set our wills on doing God's will, we can ask for anything according to His will, and it will be accomplished.

THAT'LL PREACH

Have you ever watched a baby try to get out of a crib when they are still too small? They will push the walls. They will kick their legs. They will roll against it. But the crib does not move. They will reach up. They can touch the top, but they cannot get out. The baby knows that freedom is just beyond the crib wall. They know that the barrier between them and the floor is the crib. But their knowledge cannot free them. But if that same baby cries out for their parent, and their parent comes, they can be lifted out of their situation. We should relate to God in the same way. It is not understanding our obstacle, understanding our goal, or understanding how to work that frees us. It's knowing who to call. And the quicker we call out on our Father God, the quicker we can move in the freedom God has called us too.

CONCLUSION

Jesus is the way, the truth, and the life. He gives the wisdom we need to live life well. The best wisdom is not a matter of knowing the most information. The best wisdom is a matter of knowing whom to seek for everything we need. Our knowledge cannot save us. Our knowledge alone does not help us thrive. Our knowledge cannot transform our world. But the wisdom of God can transform us and our world. Knowing information has limited impact. But knowing Jesus has limitless impact.

NOTES

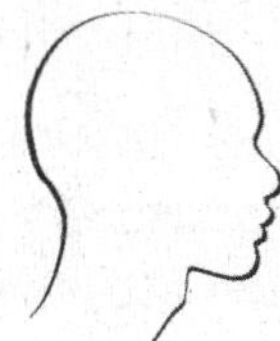

Rejoice! Endure! Pray!

By Rev. Christian Savage

Lesson Theme	Unit Theme	Scripture
Faith and Wisdom	Faith and Wisdom in James	James 1:1–11

INTRODUCTION

God is speaking to His people! The epistle of James is addressed to "the twelve tribes which are scattered abroad." James is addressing his own people, Jewish Christians, who lived outside of their ancestral homeland of Palestine. He was speaking to the Jewish Christians on the continents of Africa, Asia, and Europe. Some of them chose to migrate from Palestine in search of economic opportunities made possible by the Hellenistic and Roman Empires. But others were forced to migrate by the Assyrian and Babylonian Empires who enslaved and relocated them. Black Christians share a similar diasporic experience, and we need to hear a similar word from the Lord. Thank God, there is a word from the Lord: rejoice, endure, and pray!

MESSAGE POINTS

Message Point 1: "Rejoice!" (James 1:1)

James is a book of many moral imperatives. The first imperative is to rejoice, be glad! The Greek word translated as *greetings* literally means to rejoice. It was a common form of salutation in the ancient world, but it would be a most unusual greeting in our world. The three most common letter salutations in our society are *hi*, *dear*, or simply *greetings*. None of them elicit a reaction from the recipient. But *rejoice* calls the recipient to be glad about the communication. In this case, the writer rouses his readers to gladly receive the epistle. As his present-day readers, he urges us to receive his letter with joy even amid our own trials and temptations. Basically, he says that you can keep your joy because the trial is only a test of your faith. James seems to believe we already know that our trials are only the "testing of your faith" to produce "endurance."

Message Point 2: "Endure!" (v. 4)

What is endurance? The King James Version will translate this word as patience, but commentators of *The Interpreter's Bible* state that this translation is too passive. James intends to communicate an active resistance to the trials and temptations that beset a believer's life. Harriet Tubman demonstrated this active resistance as a conductor on the "Underground Railroad." Tubman recounted her own prayer, stating, "I said to the Lord, I'm going to hold steady on to you, and I know you will see me through." Tubman had faith that God was working on her behalf to bring an end the institution of slavery, but she did not passively wait for God to move; she actively resisted. She prayed for and received uncommon wisdom to escape to freedom by means of the "Underground Railroad" and led hundreds of other slaves to freedom as well. Active resistance is produced by faith. Believers like Tubman fight because they have faith that the battle can be won. Active resistance is the embodiment of faith. This is reflective of the main idea of the epistle of James: Behaviors should reflect beliefs in action.

Message Point 3: "Pray!" (vv. 5–9)

Harriett Tubman put her body in harm's way because she believed that her prayer would be answered and slavery would be abolished. She discovered that prayer works! According to James, prayer is how believers gain access to God's wisdom. People like Tubman who were denied an education due to their social location can approach God in prayer. The only requirement that James speaks of is faith. Without it, James declares, it is impossible to receive anything from God. Perhaps our ancestors held dearly to their faith because they needed so much from God. God was willing to do what the government was unwilling to do. God was willing to raise the poor and lower the rich. The faith of the modern Christian is that God is not done yet, but we have faith that one day, "Every valley shall be exalted, and every mountain and hill shall be made low: and the crooked shall be made straight, and the rough places plain: And the glory of the LORD shall be revealed" (from Isaiah 40:4–5).

THAT'LL PREACH

The wisdom of the ancestors is often passed through song. The Negro spirituals were originally sung by people who were legally unable to learn how to read or write. But today we hear their words of wisdom clearly in songs like *Go Down Moses*. That song is a lyrical demand for freedom from a group of people who did not have legal power, but their faith was a form of power. It was a form of power that let them endure the dark night of slavery and rise above the position of servitude. Soon after the end of slavery, many began to sing another song: "Oh freedom, oh freedom, oh freedom over me. And before I'd be a slave I'll be buried in my grave. And go home to my Lord and be free." God had given them the faith to successfully fight a war for their own emancipation, and they were not going to go back.

CONCLUSION

There is a word from the Lord. Rejoice, endure, and pray, for God is not dead! The same God who fulfilled the hope of Harriet Tubman is still alive and well. The same God who raised Himself from the dead is stilling raising our people out of poverty.

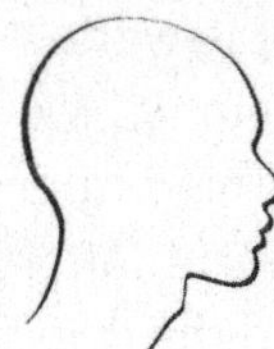

Hearing and Doing the Word

By Wayne Hopkins

Lesson Theme	Unit Theme	Scripture
Hearing and Doing the Word	Faith and Wisdom in James	James 1:19–27

INTRODUCTION

It is ironic that the two places most likely to be the site of some of the most heated, passionate, downright violent arguments would be the home and the church. In the business world people try to be civil, agreeing to disagree, and other such pleasantries. However, when we get around the folks we claim to care for the most, we tend to become far too comfortable administering tough love and laying our religion down. James is well aware that we are tempted to use our Christian status as a covering for our shortcomings while exposing those of others. We must remember to be ambassadors for Christ. This means we are not simply instructed, but we are called. If we hear the call, then we must answer not with words but with action; so what do we do now?

MESSAGE POINTS

Message Point 1: "The Need to Get Right" (James 1:19–20)

Our world has gone mad. Not in the classic sense of insanity, but in the very vulgar, vernacular sense that our society seems to feed on insult more than inspiration. Due to advances in communication and technology, we can send and receive more messages more frequently than ever. Yet, we seem to have become quicker to misinterpret, misunderstand, and misrepresent ourselves, leading us to mistreat each other. It would be interesting to see what James may have overheard from his church's conversation, or what his members may have posted on their social media. It is interesting that, despite the lack of our modern tools, the work of gossip and otherwise spreading bad news somehow was done quite thoroughly during ancient times. This lets us know that our slide into madness has been long in coming, and something that the church was designed to mitigate. Proverbs 15:1 advises that a soft answer turns away wrath. While there are many tips to try preventing and avoiding conflict, Jesus offers the most radical approach, saying that our forgiveness should be limitless (Matthew 18:22), so long as it is extended with the hope of reconciliation. James takes up the mantle, advising us that no one is above God's commandment to love. No one goes without the need to be heard and understood. Beyond this, it is the purpose, responsibility, and burden of the church to seek the best way to live in harmony. This requires us to hear, study, and actually live according to God's Word. Simply attending church is not the answer. It is the start of a process. We are not automatically granted rightness just by showing up. We must still seek first the kingdom of God and His righteousness in order to get right.

Message Point 2: "Moving into the Light"

Every element of the Christian faith represents change. Holy discipline is not wrong, but we work too hard to control the behavior of others, largely in a hypocritical way. Just as Paul called the Corinthians to examine themselves (1 Corinthians 11:28–29) in light of the Lord's Supper, James is admonishing the church to take a good look at themselves if they are to be called by the Lord's name. James says the Word is engrafted—meaning it is written on our hearts. As such, he insists that we move into the light in order to see ourselves honestly. As it stands, we have been conditioned by popular culture to hiss at the light much like fictional vampiric creatures. This is the trap of the enemy. We should not run from the light; we should crave it, desiring it with our whole hearts. After all, Jesus told us, He is the Light of the World (John 8:12). If we hear the Word and do not move toward the light, what does that say about our faith and our witness?

Message Point 3: "Pleasing in God's Sight" (v. 22)

Self-deception is a dangerous thing. Instead of looking in the mirror to check ourselves, we peer out the window, finding fault in others. Worse, we hear God's Word and consider it a suggestion rather than salvation. The psalmist cried, "Let the words of my mouth, and the meditation of my heart, be acceptable in thy sight, O LORD." We pray fervently—but it is rarely the prayer for holy speech and godly wisdom. We want knowledge that will hold others ransom. We listen to respond, not to understand. In our engagements with each other, we often forget that it is our relationship with God that should govern our connections with anyone and everyone else. We see a need and won't fulfill it. We hear calls for help but ignore them to avoid inconvenience. If we truly desire to be pleasing to God, it should be evident that we are not simply listening for God to bless us and our desires. We should be listening for His instructions that will place us where His will is to be done! If we desire to be pleasing in His sight, we must be available, and above all, be active in our pursuit of God's approval with our lives.

THAT'LL PREACH

A little girl was the apple of her father's eye. Despite Mom's protest, she was given a puppy, and it was her job to feed him and lock the gate so he could not escape. Of course, after a time, the puppy became a dog, and his feeding and care became a chore. One day the little girl screamed at the top of her lungs because she went out to feed the dog, but he was gone. She was terrified to tell her father, and decided to run away from home. As she zipped her pink backpack and headed down the road she saw her dad's car pulling into the driveway. Brokenhearted, she ran to the car and flung herself into dad's arms, sobbing. "I'm sorry but Peetey got out, and I have to run away. It's all my fault he's gone!" Just then, she heard a bark and saw her puppy bouncing out of dad's car. "I saw him down the street, and I knew what had happened. Now go feed him and lock him in, and maybe you can run away tomorrow—but not today!" No matter what we do wrong, God gives us opportunities to try again to get it right, to let our words match our actions and His will.

CONCLUSION

Obeying God's Word is not a matter of staying Christian; it's a matter of staying alive. Everything God teaches us and expects of us is entirely possible. He even promised that His yoke is easy and His burden is light. If we are weighed down, maybe it's time to listen less to the world and tune in to the Word. Truly, it never fails.

What Makes Our Faith Come Alive

By Gina A. S. Robinson

Lesson Theme	Unit Theme	Scripture
Faith Without Works Is Dead	Faith and Wisdom in James	James 2:14-26

INTRODUCTION

"Faith without works is dead" is commonly interjected in conversations among Christians, yet if we asked where to find this scriptural reference in the Bible, folks might not even know. Moreover, some folks cannot even fully explain what this phrase means to them or how it functions in their faith. Yet there is truth wrapped up in this statement. In other letters, Paul teaches that our works will not make us righteous. In today's text, it seems like James is teaching the opposite of Paul, but he is actually making a supportive point. Paul and James are talking about two different types of work. Paul's idea of "works" includes following the ancient Jewish laws, such as circumcision, as a way of showing one is faithful to God. James' idea of "works" focuses on actions, such as charity, that allow us to exercise what we believe. Essentially, James argues that the best way to show people what you believe is by putting our faith in action. Our work in the church, our communities, and throughout the body of Christ lets the world know that our faith is not dead. This text highlights three actions that make our faith come alive.

MESSAGE POINTS

Message Point 1: "Serving Others Makes Our Faith Come Alive" (James 2:14–19)

Serving others makes our faith come alive. James asks a series of questions beginning with, "What doth it profit, my brethren, though a man say he hath faith, and have not works?" James follows this question up with an example of how a person, who believes their faith alone makes them righteous, would treat a neighbor if she or he were hungry or cold. Granting the person in need well-wishes does nothing to meet their bodily need. In this case, "faith, if it hath not works, is dead." James teaches us that serving others makes our faith come alive. Faith alone does not require us to be in a relationship with others. Faith alone does not require us to serve others. However, the work of serving people calls us to form connections with people during moments of vulnerability. Serving others moves us from the inactive position of a member of the church to the active position of a servant of the most high God. Serving others resurrects a dead faith and makes it come alive.

Message Point 2: "Sacrifice Makes Our Faith Come Alive" (vv. 20–24)

Sacrifice makes our faith come alive. James offers an event from the narrative of Abraham's life as an example of faith and works operating together. As you know, Abraham offered his son on the altar as an act of his faith in God. Sacrificing his son meant that he was also willing to sacrifice the future of his family's existence. This display of radical faith coupled with the radical action or work of sacrificing his son was met with God's radical response. James states in verse 22, "Seest thou how faith wrought with his works, and by works was faith made perfect?" Abraham's faith was brought to completion when he sacrificed the ram that appeared in the bush in place of his son. His faith would not have been brought to completion if he was not willing to sacrifice his son. While sacrificing a child is an extreme example, what are you willing to sacrifice to make your faith come alive? Sacrifice is a work of faith, because it calls us into a space of vulnerability in which we must depend on God. In those moments of vulnerability, God shows up, and our faith comes alive.

Message Point 3: "Showing Hospitality Makes Our Faith Come Alive" (vv. 25–26)

Last, showing hospitality makes our faith come alive. In verse 24, James states, "Ye see then how that by works a man is justified, and not by faith only." Not only does the narrative of Abraham provide an example illuminating this truth, but so does the lesser known narrative of Rahab. Rahab also demonstrated how faith and works operate together when she offered radical hospitality to the spies by welcoming them in her home. Welcoming people who are unlike us into our personal space is a work of faith because we must trust that the Holy Spirit will mediate the interaction. Showing hospitality to people who are unlike us through both intentional and organic encounters creates an opportunity for our faith to come alive. The Spirit shows up in the midst of this act of faith and aids in fostering divine connections among souls. James' concludes his argument about faith and works as he coordinates works with the soul and faith with the body, because works and the soul keep the faith and the body alive. Therefore, "faith without works is dead" makes good sense. Showing hospitality is a work that makes our faith come alive.

THAT'LL PREACH

Around this time of the year, many high school students are preparing to embark on the first leg of their journey into adulthood. Some go to college or trade school, while others join the military or get a job. Whichever path they choose, each of them had to put in some work before taking their first step on this particular course. Students have to work hard in the classroom, military personnel take tests, and employees fill out applications. These teenagers could have all the faith in the world, but without putting in some work, their dreams would never come true. Their work and faith create the possibility of opening a new chapter in their lives as young adults. Our teenagers show us not only how our faith comes alive, but also how dreams come true when we put in the work in our own lives.

CONCLUSION

Faith without works is dead; therefore, we must act if we want to make our faith come alive. Serving others, sacrificing, and showing hospitality are three ways to make our faith come alive, but there are many more. Believing in God and God's Word is important; however, connecting with God's people through our works is what makes us disciples. So if you know that you are a person who is filled with faith but does not want to work on behalf of others or yourself, then I encourage you to *get to work* and make your faith come alive.

Words Have Meaning and Consequences

By Emmanuel Ephraim, MDiv, MTS

Lesson Theme	Unit Theme	Scripture
Taming the Tongue	Faith and Wisdom in James	James 3:1–12

INTRODUCTION

The words we speak reveal the intent of our minds and have consequences. Jesus warns us that people will give account for every careless word they speak, "for by your words you will be justified, and by your words you will be condemned" (Matthew 12:36–37). All words have consequences. We all must assume responsibility for the words we use. We must delete all unsavory and all unbecoming speech from our utterances.

MESSAGE POINTS

Message Point 1: "Our Words Influence Others" (James 3:1–5)

The church must not appoint just anyone to be teachers in the house of the Lord (v. 1). Those who teach have greater accountability because their words influence others more than mere conversational speech. Potentially we all fail from time to time or use incorrect language in our speech (v. 2.) The aim is to so train your mind that you do not utter any unsavory or unedifying words. That is the way to tame the tongue. Examples in daily life show that discipline and training are necessary for a life that edifies and glorifies the Lord (vv. 3–5). Horses need bridles to guide them, and ships need rudders to steer them. How then do we now use the tongue to steer us toward purposeful and intentional speech that edifies rather sets ablaze emotions in our relationships?

Message Point 2: "Our Words Inflict Wounds On Others" (vv. 6–8)

You have heard the childish rhyme "sticks and stones may break my bones, but words will never hurt me." That proves to be so false in real life. From God's point of view, our words reveal the content of our minds. Our words tend to reveal the state of our unrighteous minds (v. 6a), and our words tend to reveal the path of unrighteousness affecting our environment and relationships in the direction of hell itself (v. 6b). The humanity of all tribes has found a way to tame all kinds of creatures of the air, land, and sea (v. 7), but no human has ever learned to control his speech for only beneficial purposes. Instead human speech continues to spew out vile, violent, destructive, and hurtful words that tear us apart (v. 8).

Message Point 3: "Our Words Insult The Dignity Of Others" (vv. 9–12)

Is it not hypocritical that our speech can be used to sing praises to God and yet also be used to demean our fellow human beings made in the image of God (v. 9)? It is a contradiction of the wholesomeness within ourselves when we do things like that (v. 10). Such contradictions do not occur in nature (vv. 11–12), so why do we allow it to happen in us, those who claim to be born again and have a new nature in Christ?

THAT'LL PREACH

FCC regulations used to prohibit the use of foul language over public radio airwaves. All radio stations were held to this strict regulation and were levied a fine for each instance of violation. To avoid the violation of the regulations, most talk radio shows incorporated a six-second delay into their broadcasts. This gave the producer enough time to "bleep" out any inadvertent use of language before the broadcast is released on the airwaves. Like talk radio stations, we must have a six-second delay between our brains and our tongues. We must not let our speech be anything that pops into our minds.

CONCLUSION

Begin to eradicate bad language from your daily speech (Ephesians 4:2–9). Build up your vocabulary with meaningful words so you do not have to fall back on the same old worthless speech. Have a dictionary handy or an app on your phone. Read some good Christian books regularly. This is the process that will lead you to what Paul exhorted us to "be ye transformed by the renewing of your mind, that ye may prove what is the good and acceptable and perfect will of God" (Romans 12:2). We know it is important. We have the sources at hand. Now let's do it!

NOTES

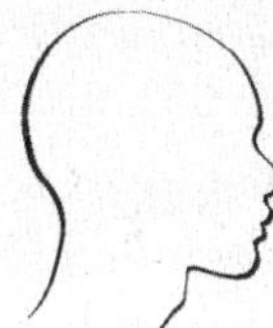

Wisdom as Walking Faith

By Jeremias Santos

Lesson Theme	Unit Theme	Scripture
Two Kinds of Wisdom	Faith and Wisdom in James	James 3:13–18; 5:7–12

INTRODUCTION

The Scripture here contains a small part of the dialogue between James and his audience of believers. It contains elements that are repeated throughout the book: being boastful, issues of anger, partiality, endurance, patience, faith and works, the poor and the rich, sin giving birth to death, and God's word giving birth to us as the first fruits of His new creation. Faith and wisdom become keystones to understanding this dialogue. James shows us how those who live with true, vibrant faith are those who live with true wisdom, grounded in peace and patience.

MESSAGE POINTS

Message Point 1: "Who Is Wise Among You?" (James 3:13, 17–18)

For James, moving beyond a statement of faith means that one's actions have meaning in the here and now. Our faith is lived out, and the result is growth in wisdom. The "wisdom from above" for James, which is lived out through works, is always rooted in peace. What we do should be done peacefully and should result in peace. This peace is not simply the end of the process but an environment in which the community acts: in mercy, in kindness, without partiality, without envy, without feeling like being rich or poor has any meaning, without concern for status. In such an environment, everyone is able to grow in wisdom, and everyone is equally enabled to contribute to the community: it is a harvest of righteousness sown in peace.

Message Point 2: "Wisdom That Is Not Wisdom" (James 3:14; 5:9)

These verses indicate that some of the tension in the churches James addresses has to do with a disparity between rich and poor in the congregations and the envy it can engender. A good part of James comes back to distinctions between the lives of the rich and poor. Anger surfaces when envy becomes part of your perspective: Why do I not have more? Why *should* I not have more? Why is God blessing that person and not me? Envy may be a reason some seek to become teachers in the church—to gain influence or status. James addresses an audience of believers in which some are being tempted to seek the appearance of wisdom at the expense of the truth. They seek positions that seem powerful but which bear an enormous responsibility in the community. This is "wisdom" that *is not* wisdom. If we desire selfish gain, there is no consideration for how it affects others, only what advances our cause. This kind of selfish ambition leads to sin, death, and destruction of a community.

Message Point 3: "It Is the Path That Leads You There" (James 5:7–8, 10–11)

Obtaining wisdom and growing in it requires patience and time. Living in a community that is faithful to Christ's calling will inevitably lead to times of suffering. But such times are needed. James uses the analogy of a farmer and the need for patience. The farmer does not simply wait for the crop but is "patient *with* it." This is critical in understanding how wisdom operates and how it leads to more wisdom: the farmer has to decide *not* to plow under his field, *not* to start over, but instead to wait for the late rains, which might or might not come. The analogy here emphasizes that patience is rewarded and that experience will lead to wisdom reliant on God, not on control. Since the history of a people is important to understanding their identity, James constructs a path forward for the Christian communities that are increasingly adding Gentiles to their population of Jews. Jews felt threatened because the Gentiles did not share their traditions, while Gentiles felt left out because they didn't share the Jewish religious history. James is showing them that the very real difficulties they face together require them to respond with a patience that will bring them and bind them together. The examples of Job and the prophets hearken back to that ancient history that identifies a people called by God but also to an understanding that even the prophets were not spared suffering, but brought closer to God because of it.

THAT'LL PREACH

There are so many examples of congregations, or even nonprofits and community groups, that are struggling with the same issues. Do you know of one? Do you know of someone who is an interim pastor at a church having to be James? Many community leaders struggle with their community's identity and selfish ambition from members who are more concerned with their status than the health of the community. You are called to be James in your community. You have the responsibility to lead with peace and to guide toward peace. You have an opportunity to remind your community members who they are and to point out the wise among them. Their struggles are not a sign of disfavor, but a point in history they share with past generations and individuals, like Job and the prophets.

CONCLUSION

The book of James makes a distinction between two kinds of wisdom. One kind comes from selfish desires based on envy and selfish ambition. Whether specifically ambition for monetary gain or for influence and status, this is the kind of wisdom that gives birth to sin and death. It means that the results will be to achieve success at the price of others.

The wisdom that comes from God, however, is not simply concerned with a world that is yet to come, a spirituality that is disconnected from our lives. Instead, God's wisdom connects and binds us together in a value system that requires acts of love, genuine kindness, thoughtfulness, and joyful thankfulness. These values—and the fruit they bear—allow us to truly grow in grace and peace as a community because we are lifted up together.

Notes

Notes

Notes

Notes

Notes

Notes